Wild
DRINKS
and COCKTAILS

Quarto is the authority on a wide range of topics.

Quarto educates, entertains and enriches the lives of
our readers—enthusiasts and lovers of hands-on living.

www.quartoknows.com

First published in the United States of America in 2016 by
Fair Winds Press, a member of
Quarto Publishing Group USA Inc.
100 Cummings Center
Suite 406-L
Beverly, Massachusetts 01915-6101
Telephone: (978) 282-9590
Fax: (978) 283-2742
QuartoKnows.com
Visit our blogs at QuartoKnows.com

20 19 18 17 16   1 2 3 4 5

ISBN: 978-1-59233-707-1

Digital edition published in 2015
eISBN: 978-1-62788-757-1

Library of Congress Cataloging-in-Publication Data available

Cover and interior design by Amanda Richmond
Photography by Emily Han and Gregory Han, except for page 185 by Shane Redsar.

Printed and bound in China

The information in this book is for educational purposes only. It is not intended to replace
the advice of a physician or medical practitioner. Please see your health care provider before
beginning any new health program.

Wild
DRINKS
and COCKTAILS

HANDCRAFTED SQUASHES,
SHRUBS, SWITCHELS, TONICS, AND
INFUSIONS TO MIX AT HOME

EMILY HAN

FAIR WINDS

CONTENTS

INTRODUCTION

WHAT DO I SEE WHEN I POUR MYSELF A GLASS OF ELDERFLOWER cordial? Its fresh, pale-yellow hue reminds me of the gnarled yet resilient elder tree rooted in a sunny hillside near my home, and its taste makes me think of the warm spring morning when I gathered the creamy white blossoms in the company of bees, and how I spent hours sitting on my balcony, steadily and quietly plucking the flowers from their stems. It puts me in mind of deer and squirrels, too, for the elder tree provides them with shelter and forage. A few months after the elder tree blooms, its fragrant flowers will turn into clusters of juicy purple berries: food for songbirds and delicious medicine for my friends and family. Each sip of elderflower cordial contains an entire natural world—sun, air, water, earth, animals, and insects—and there are generations of people in that world, too, such as herbalists, cooks, teachers, and students. And, if you ask me, that's nothing short of magical.

I began wildcrafting about ten years ago. Although I grew up with nature-loving, plant-growing, herbal medicine–practicing parents, it wasn't until I moved to one of the largest urban areas in the world that I really started interacting with wild plants: and, by extension, wild drinks. It may seem surprising that I discovered nature in the middle of Los Angeles—but nature is everywhere you look, from the elder tree around the corner to the mallows growing in sidewalk cracks and the feral pomegranates that dwell in empty lots. As I've discovered, connecting with nature or becoming a forager or wildcrafter doesn't mean you have to live on umpteen acres in the countryside (though it's lovely if you do!). The truth is, wherever we live, we have access to nourishment and inspiration. And I channeled my inspiration into making drinks. That's because I fell in love with the bounty of seasonal ingredients available in my new city, and I wanted new

ways to play with all the tastes, smells, and colors I encountered in the world around me. (Also, making drinks involves lots of bottles and jars, which *might* be a slight obsession of mine.) I love being able to turn the berries I gather in the morning into a unique cocktail that same evening—and I love sharing my handcrafted drinks with others, because they've got a unique power to make any gathering or celebration a bit more special.

As I explored wild foods and beverage-making, I became increasingly fascinated by the connection between drinks and medicine. So many teas, syrups, vinegars, liqueurs, and other drinks have their roots (no pun intended!) in herbal medicine, which has been practiced by grandmothers, monks, and physicians alike over the centuries. As I learned about the herbs, roots, seeds, and fruits that I found growing near me, I discovered that many of them weren't just delicious: they could also be called upon to soothe a stomachache, calm a stressed-out mind, or support a flagging immune system. We often look to "super-foods" that grow in far-off places to boost our health, but why should we ignore the powerful and nutritious medicinal plants—often known pejoratively as "weeds"—that are growing right on our doorsteps? What's more, the process of making our own drinks and herbal remedies is just as important as the end result: it's healing and empowering in itself.

People are often surprised to learn that botanical treasures such as elderflowers are flourishing in their local environments—even in cities. Although this book is a collection of recipes, not a field guide, I hope it'll inspire you to learn about and interact with the place where you live. Also, because I know that not everyone has easy access to every single ingredient, in these recipes I've made an effort to use plants that can also be grown in a garden, found at the farmers' market, and made with dried herbs instead of fresh ones. Plus, I've included a list of high-quality mail-order sources in the Resources on page 182, and I hope you'll find it helpful.

Wild Drinks begins with a primer on wildcrafting and a run-down of some of the ingredients, tools, and techniques you'll use in wild drink making. From there, it explores different types of drinks—from teas, juices, and lemonades to syrups and squashes, and from vinegar-based drinks to infused liquors and wines, and lots more. In many of the recipes, I share information on how different plants are used as herbal remedies. This can be tricky, because true—and truly effective—herbal medicine is complex, nuanced, and personalized, and can't be reduced to general statements like, "Use this herb to fix that ailment." That said, I'm sharing these tidbits in the hope that they'll encourage you to learn more. I hope this book will inspire you to explore the wild ingredients that grow in your neighborhood—and to experiment with the flavors that speak to you. *Salut*!

Disclaimer

THIS BOOK IS AN EDUCATIONAL and informational resource. It is not given as medical advice and is not a substitute for working with a health care practitioner. If you have an existing medical condition, are taking medications, are pregnant or breastfeeding, or otherwise need medical or herbal advice, consult your health care practitioner. The author and publisher assume no responsibility for adverse reactions or sensitivities to ingredients. You are responsible for educating yourself about food safety and making sure you have correctly identified any wild food before picking or ingesting it.

CHAPTER 1

CRAFTING WILD DRINKS

An Introduction to Wildcrafting

WILDCRAFTING IS THE PRACTICE OF GATHERING WILD OR UNCULTIvated plants and using them to make food, drink, or medicine. That might sound like a synonym for foraging, but I like the word *wildcrafting* because it encompasses the creative part of the process. A term frequently used by herbalists, *wildcrafting* also implies the development of a relationship with a place, as opposed to a haphazard rummaging around. And that takes care, attention, and time. Wildcrafters are respectful of the entire ecosystem: we practice sustainable and ethical foraging by considering the long-term health of the plants, animals, and people that comprise that ecosystem. In other words, when you practice wildcrafting, you aren't just picking free berries to make a cocktail; you're also being mindful of the following issues:

- Can you correctly identify the plant? Are you 100 percent sure?

- Do you have permission to gather the plant?

- How abundant or rare is the plant? Is it endangered, native, invasive?

- Is the plant free from contamination such as pesticides, insecticides, fertilizers, auto pollution, agricultural and manufacturing waste, and dog pee?

- Is the plant population healthy?

- Are there animals that depend on this plant for food or shelter?

- Will your actions kill a plant, prevent it from reproducing, or leave it vulnerable to disease?

- Are you harvesting only what you need?

- How can you give back to the ecosystem in a positive way?

The answers to these questions might not be immediately obvious. To help you tune in to them, try this: before you start foraging, find any green space at all, such as a garden, a lone weed poking up through the cracks in the sidewalk, or even the flowerpot that's sitting on your balcony or outside your front door. Find a plant—any plant will do—and sit with it for a while. What do you notice about the shape of its leaves, the pattern of its petals, or the way it smells?

Now get to know the world around the plant. Does it thrive in the warm sun or cool shade? What is its water source? Do you hear any insects, birds, or other animals? Being able to slow down and use your senses will serve you well when you learn to identify edible plants, because you may need to visit and observe a spot many times before you go home with anything. That's part of the process, and it's a plus: your wild drinks will be even more satisfying when you finally start harvesting. (Of course, if your backyard looks like a huge field of dandelions, you can probably safely pick as many as you like.)

To learn how to properly identify plants, you'll want a good field guide (or three) to your area, plus a book on foraging in general to help you start learning about the most common and abundant plants. (Need a few suggestions? Visit the Resources section on pages 182 and 183.) And, if possible, seek out an experienced local wildcrafter who can teach you how to identify and use the plants that grow in your region throughout the seasons. Getting in touch with a regional herbalist is often one of the best ways to do just that.

And, before you learn how to identify local edibles, find out which plants in your region are fatally poisonous, such as poison hemlock and water hemlock, and which plants may cause allergic reactions, such as poison ivy, poison oak, and poison sumac. This caution isn't intended to make you afraid of your environment: knowing these things will actually make you more comfortable and confident as you explore. Field guides, native plant societies, your state's university extension office, and university agriculture or botany departments are all good resources.

This might sound like a lot of work, but trust me: it's completely worth it, because it'll make your wild drinks even more pleasurable. And setting aside contemporary culture's instant-gratification mentality in favor of developing a meaningful relationship with the natural world can be so rewarding. Your family and friends will appreciate it, too, when you share the delicious fruits of your labors.

The Basics of Harvesting

IN ADDITION TO KNOWING WHAT YOU'RE PICKING, IT'S IMPORTANT TO pay close attention to *where* you're picking, and to avoid plants that may have been sprayed with chemicals or exposed to contaminants in the air, soil, or water. To that end, avoid harvesting along busy roadsides, golf courses, and industrial areas.

Check out the area before you start harvesting. Move around so that you don't just pick the first plant you see; it might be the only one around (in which case you should leave it alone), or there might be better specimens farther along. Figure out which plants are older, younger, healthier, or less healthy: in some cases, it's fine to pick tender young greens, while in other cases, it might be more prudent to leave a seedling alone so it can mature. Try to spread yourself around: pluck here and there and avoid overharvesting from a single plant or plant population. And remember to express gratitude in any way that feels right to you, whether it's thanking the plant, spreading seeds for the next generation, picking up trash, or participating in nature protection efforts.

WHAT ARE YOU LOOKING FOR WHEN YOU'RE HARVESTING?

• **Leaves are usually harvested in spring and summer;** they often have the best flavor and highest levels of essential oils just before the plant flowers. Pick leaves gently, using your fingers or pruning shears, and shake them to remove any insects that might be clinging to them. I also like to check the undersides of leaves before I pick them, because insects sometimes lay their eggs there. (It's not that I'm squeamish: I just like to be mindful of the insects.)

• **Flowers are usually harvested just before or after they bloom.** As you would with leaves, pick flowers gently using your fingers or pruning shears, and shake them to remove insects. (You can also lay them out on a cloth for an hour or so, and wait for the insects to crawl away.) Be aware that when you harvest a flower, you're preventing it from being pollinated, fruiting, and going to seed—thus, you're limiting the availability of fruits and seeds for yourself, or local wildlife, at a later date.

• **Fruits and berries are usually harvested in summer or fall.** Encountering free fruit can be particularly exciting, and sometimes we get greedy, and end up taking more than we need. Consider how much fruit you can reasonably process and eat in order to prevent food waste, and be mindful that birds and other animals may need the berries for food.

• **Seeds and nuts are usually harvested in late summer or fall.** Techniques vary depending on the plant, but one way to collect seeds is to shake them into a bag. For flowers, you can tap the seed head into an open bag to catch the tumbling seeds; for pinecones, you can shake and tap the cone with a stick to dislodge the nuts.

When and where it's appropriate, spread the seeds to encourage future plant populations. Remember that seeds and nuts allow plants to reproduce, and they're often food for birds and mammals.

• **Roots are usually harvested in late summer or fall,** after the plant has gone to seed. Certain roots can also be harvested in spring and others, such as burdock, should be harvested in the plant's first year. Depending on the size of the root, you might need to use anything from a small soil knife to a larger gardening shovel to harvest it. And be aware that when you harvest a root, you may be killing the plant it sustains.

USEFUL HARVESTING TOOLS

• **Your hands will do most of the work of gathering plants.** In some cases—such as when you're gathering stinging nettles—you'll want to protect them with gardening gloves.

• **Use pruning shears for clipping plants that you can't pinch off with your fingers.**

• **A fruit picker is useful for reaching fruits on tall trees.**

• **Use a soil knife or hori-hori for digging roots, such as dandelion roots.**

• **Carry paper or cloth bags for holding plant material.** (Avoid plastic bags, which don't allow plant material to breathe: they lead to fast wilting.)

• **Consider bringing a basket for holding plant material when practical.** (What conditions constitute "practical"? Well, gathering in your backyard is practical; hiking 10 miles with your basket in tow is probably not.)

• **Other useful supplies include a hat, to protect your face and head from the sun;** long pants and long sleeves, if there's any danger of encountering poison oak, poison ivy, thorns, snakes, or ticks; a bottle of water and a snack; a field guide or plant identification guide; a notebook; a camera; and a first-aid kit.

In the Kitchen

INGREDIENTS

Fruits and Vegetables

MAKING WILD DRINKS IS ALL ABOUT CAPTURING THE FLAVORS of a season, so use fruits and vegetables when they're at their peak. Although you should always choose produce that's free from decay, most of the time you'll be mashing, infusing, or altering it in such a way that its outward appearance isn't that important. At the farmers' market, ask growers whether they have "seconds"— cheaper fruits and vegetables that may look imperfect, but that taste just as good as the prettier ones.

One exception to the in-season rule is berries. When berries are picked at peak season and are quickly frozen after picking,

most of them will work just as well as fresh berries in drink recipes, and they'll last for up to one year in the freezer. To freeze fresh berries, spread them in a single layer on a parchment-paper-lined tray and pop them in the freezer; then, transfer the frozen berries to a freezer-safe bag or container. (If you plan to store your berries in rigid glass or plastic containers, leave an inch [2.5 cm] of headspace, because foods may expand during freezing.) To use frozen berries, thaw them first, and include the juices in whatever you are making.

Use unwaxed and organically grown produce whenever possible, especially when it comes to citrus fruits such as oranges and lemons, which you'll use for peels. Many recipes call for wide strips of citrus peel, which are easy to cut using a vegetable peeler. (Take care to avoid the bitter white pith underneath. Scrape off any remaining bits of pith with a paring knife.) When a recipe calls for grated citrus peel, use a Microplane grater or a box grater with fine holes.

Herbs

Whether they've been harvested outdoors or bought from a store, fresh herbs should look crisp and vibrant, not limp or dry. Store soft leafy herbs, such as basil or mint, in a glass of water, like cut flowers. Wrap woody herbs such as rosemary and thyme in a cloth or paper towel and refrigerate in an airtight container. If you need to rinse herbs, do so gently, then pat them dry with a towel.

Dried herbs should be fragrant, crisp, and dry with no signs of mold. Store them in airtight containers away from heat, moisture, and light, and refresh them about once a year. To dry your own herbs, loosely tie them in small bundles and hang them upside down in a well-ventilated spot away from direct sunlight. When the herbs have thoroughly dried (about 1 to 2 weeks), strip off the leaves or flowers for storage. To prevent the herbs from getting dusty, tear holes in the side of a paper bag to allow for airflow, and then use it to cover the herbs. You can also dry herbs in a dehydrator set to low (95° to 115°F [35° to 46°C]); depending upon the herb, this takes anywhere from 1 to 4 hours.

In most recipes that call for fresh herbs, you can substitute dried herbs; simply use half the amount the recipe calls for. Likewise, if you're substituting fresh herbs for dried, double the amount indicated in the recipe.

Finally, when purchasing herbs, do your research first, and buy from sources that support organic and sustainable farming and ethical wildcrafting. (Check out the Resources on pages 182 and 183 for ideas.)

Spices

Most of the recipes in this book call for whole spices, which retain their flavor far longer than ground or powdered ones. (They've got another advantage, too: they're also easier to strain out of your drinks.) If it's at all possible, try to smell spices before you buy them; fragrance is a good indicator of freshness. Store spices in airtight containers away from heat, moisture, and light, and refresh them about once a year. When a recipe calls for cracking or crushing spices, use a rolling pin, a mortar and pestle, or the bottom of a sturdy jar. For grinding, use a mortar and pestle, or a small electric coffee grinder that's reserved for spices only.

Sweeteners

Sugar and other sweeteners are used for taste, texture, and sometimes to aid in preservation. In the recipes that follow, I've indicated the sweetener that I think tastes best, or that provides the most consistent results. However, unless otherwise noted, most recipes can be adapted to use any sweetener you prefer, and you can feel free to sweeten more or less to taste.

- **White sugar or granulated sugar** is an all-purpose refined sugar made from sugarcane or beets. It provides the most neutral sweetness, color, and clarity in drinks.

- **Raw cane sugar or organic cane sugar** is not significantly different from white sugar, although it can make your drink darker in color. It is slightly less processed, and may contain a trace amount of molasses.

- **Brown sugar** is a refined sugar with added molasses for color and flavor.

- **Turbinado and demerara sugars** are partially refined sugars made from evaporated cane juice. They lend a richer flavor and darker color to drinks.

- **Muscovado sugar** is a partially refined sugar made from evaporated cane juice. It is dark and sticky and has a robust, molasses-like flavor.

- **Sucanat or rapadura** is an unrefined sugar made from dehydrated cane juice. It has a deep molasses flavor and color.

- **Piloncillo or panela** is an unrefined cane sugar with a molasses flavor; it's often used in Latin America.

- **Jaggery** is a raw or slightly refined sugar made from the sugar palm or sugarcane; it's often used in South Asia.

- **Palm sugar** is a raw sugar made from the sugar palm or date palm, and it's most often used in Southeast Asia.

- **Coconut sugar** is a raw sugar made from evaporated coconut palm flower sap, and its taste is similar to that of brown sugar.

- **Date sugar** is made from dehydrated, ground dates.

- **Honey** ranges in color and flavor from mild varieties, like clover and orange blossom, to bolder varieties such as buckwheat honey, which tastes malty and molasses-y.

Seek out honey varietals that are local to your area: you'll get to experiment with flavors that way, and plus, you'll be supporting the important work of local beekeepers and bees. (Local honey can even help prevent seasonal allergies!) I use raw, local honey in most of my drink making—but honey isn't always the right choice for every drink, because it can be strongly flavored and can make liquids appear cloudy. Keep in mind that honey is sweeter than sugar, so when making substitutions, start with a ratio of $^3/_4$ cup (255 g) honey to 1 cup (200 g) sugar. (And remember that you shouldn't give honey to infants younger than 1 year old.)

- **Molasses** is a liquid by-product from sugar production that retains the vitamins and minerals of the sugarcane or sugar beets from which it's made. (Blackstrap molasses is the most nutritious version.) Although molasses is less sweet than sugar, it has a strong, earthy flavor, and some varieties might even taste slightly bitter.

- **Maple syrup**, is made from the sap of the sugar maple tree. Because of its distinctive taste, it's best when it's used as a flavorful accent rather than a full substitute for sugar.

- **Maple sugar** is also made from the sugar maple, by boiling its sap until nearly all the water has evaporated. Use it with care when making substitutions because it's twice as sweet as white sugar.

- **Agave nectar** is a sweet, neutral-tasting syrup made from the agave plant.

Although it was once championed as a healthier alternative to sugar because it has a lower glycemic index, it's actually highly refined. If you choose to use it, try diluting it with an equal volume of warm water, and use it in cocktails instead of simple syrup.

• **Stevia** is an herbal sweetener made from *Stevia rebaudiana* leaves. I'm not a huge fan of its bitter aftertaste, but some people love it—especially because it has an insignificant effect on blood glucose levels, which makes it a great substitute for people with diabetes and hypoglycemia. Stevia powder is up to 300 times sweeter than sugar, so use it sparingly.

TOOLS

Never fear: you don't need a lot of special equipment to make your own drinks! In fact, you probably have most of these supplies in your kitchen already. It's helpful to have the following on hand:

• **Glass jars with tight-fitting lids for infusing and storing drinks.** Canning jars are nice and durable; get ahold of an assortment of pint (470 ml), quart (1 L), and ½-gallon (2 L) sizes. You can also reuse jars from foods like jam and pickles, but avoid reusing lids that have lingering odors. (You don't want that luscious liqueur to taste like pickles!) Some recipes call for leaving a certain amount of headspace in a jar when you're filling it;

this refers to the space between the top of the food or liquid and the inside of the jar lid.

- **Bottles with tight-fitting caps for storing juices, syrups, liqueurs, and lots more.** Swing-top or Grolsch-style bottles are sturdy, attractive, and relatively cheap. (See page 161 for tips on how to bottle fermented drinks.)

- **Fine-mesh strainer for straining liquids.** Use stainless steel or plastic, and avoid aluminum or other reactive metals. Although you can get by with just a single strainer, it's handy to have a couple: a small one for filtering teas and other liquids in small quantities, plus a large one that can easily fit over a large bowl. When you're straining, you can help guide the liquid through the strainer by gently stirring it with a spoon. If a recipe asks you to, you can also use a wooden spoon to press on the solids, to extract more liquid; however, some recipes caution against that, because it can make the final product cloudy.

- **Fine-mesh bag or cloth for straining liquids.** When a strainer isn't fine enough, or when you *really* need to squeeze the liquid out of plant material, try using a jelly bag, nut milk bag, or flour sack towel. (Skip the cheesecloth; it can be a pain to clean and reuse.) Before filtering, pour boiling water through the bag or cloth to sterilize it and help the liquid pass through more easily. Wash the bag or cloth between uses to prevent the transfer of unwanted flavors.

- **Paper coffee filters for straining liquids that carry fine sediment.** Before you start, pour boiling water through the filter to sterilize it and help the liquid pass through more easily. Consider using paper coffee filters, which are also helpful for covering fermentation jars.

- **Funnel for filling bottles mess-free.** You might want to invest in a wide-mouth funnel, which is great for filling jars.

- **Bottle brush for keeping bottles** and jars squeaky clean.

- **Pots and pans with lids**, including a small saucepan; a medium saucepan; and a stockpot. As always, use stainless steel, enamel, or glass, and avoid aluminum or other reactive metals.

- **Measuring tools**, including measuring cups and spoons. If you already have it, a digital scale can be useful, but it's not essential to the process.

- **Stirring tools**, including a large wooden spoon, a large stainless steel or plastic spoon, and a chopstick or skewer.

- **Chef's knife** for chopping various fruits and herbs.

- **Potato masher**, or another mashing tool, for crushing fruits.

- **Vegetable peeler** for peeling citrus.

- **Microplane zester** or box grater with fine holes for grating a variety of citrus peels and fresh ginger.

- **Citrus reamer or lemon squeezer** for juicing citrus fruits.

- **Rolling pin** for bruising herbs and cracking spices.

- **A spice-grinding tool**, such as a mortar and pestle or a coffee grinder.

- **Cocktail-making tools**, including a cocktail shaker, jigger, muddler, strainer, and bar spoon.

- **Appliances such as a blender, food processor, juicer, and dehydrator** are rarely necessary, but it can't do any harm to have them on hand.

- **Labels.** Because you *will* forget what's in that jar at the back of the fridge! I use extremely advanced technology here: masking tape and a permanent marker.

- **A notebook,** because you *will* want to remember and recreate that amazing liqueur. So be sure to take copious notes as you try out recipes and experiment in the kitchen.

CLEANING, SANITIZING, AND STERILIZING

Before you get going, always make sure your hands, tools, and containers are clean. At the very least, wash bottles and jars in hot, soapy water and rinse them well. Taking the extra step of sterilizing your containers will help prevent contamination by microorganisms, reduce the chances of unwanted flavors, and frequently extend the shelf life of your projects. To sterilize a glass jar or bottle, place it in a deep pot and cover it completely with water. Bring

the water to a boil over high heat. Once it reaches a full, rolling boil, continue to boil for 15 minutes, and then turn off the heat. The container may be left in the water for up to 1 hour. Remove the container using canning jar lifters or tongs, and pour out any excess water. Then, shake out excess water and fill the container promptly: don't dry it with a towel first, because that can introduce unwanted microorganisms.

You can also sanitize glass or plastic containers by rinsing them with an acid-based sanitizing solution (follow the instructions on the bottle). A chlorine bleach solution ($^1/_4$ teaspoon of bleach to 1 quart [940 ml] of water) can also be used to sanitize containers, but it shouldn't be used when making fermented drinks, because bleach can kill the yeasts that are necessary for fermentation.

YIELDS

Most of the recipes in this book yield fairly small quantities, and there are two reasons for this. First, as an urban apartment dweller, my kitchen (and fridge) space is limited, and I prefer to make a wide variety of drinks in small quantities. (Who needs 5 gallons [19 L] of rose hip syrup, anyway?) Second, I love to play and experiment: I want to encourage you to do the same, and smaller yields can free you up to be more creative. That said, most of the recipes can easily be scaled up if you're the lucky recipient of a windfall of foraged fruit, or if you want to make larger quantities for gift-giving or entertaining.

Now that you know the basics, it's time to get started making your own wild drinks!

CHAPTER 2

TEAS, JUICES, AND LEMONADES

A S SIMPLE AS IT IS POWERFUL, THERE'S NOTHING QUITE LIKE A cup of herbal tea. Served hot, it can warm your insides (and your hands); served chilled, it can refresh and reinvigorate. Tea can relax you, wake you up, soothe an upset stomach, or calm an anxious mind. What's more, making herbal tea is an easy, accessible, and inexpensive way to get to know and love your local plants—from the bunch of mint in your CSA box to the dandelion roots that your neighbor happily lets you dig up from her backyard. Before you use an herb to make other drinks, such as sodas or liqueurs, get acquainted with it by turning it into a tea. That way, you'll have a sense of how it tastes and how it makes you feel. And, when you make them yourself from fresh ingredients, fruit-based teas and juices are also a revelation, so beware: you may never drink store-bought juice again!

Basic Infusion

Basic Decoction

Herbal tea has, of course, been with us since time immemorial. In China, its existence dates back at least 4,000 years, and it continues to play an important role in traditional Chinese medicine. Ancient Egyptian documents also mention herbal tea, and the ancient Greeks enjoyed it as well: that's why teas made from herbs other than the tea bush (*Camellia sinensis*) are more properly called "tisanes," a word that originates from the Greek *ptisane*, or a drink made from pearl barley. (In a tribute to its Greek heritage, a modern version of the *ptisane* can be found on page 44.)

Herbal teas are made using two different techniques, which herbalists call "infusions" and "decoctions." That might sound complicated, but it it's actually really easy to make herbal, medicinal teas that are also great foundations for other flavorful drinks, such as syrups (chapter 3) and sodas (chapter 7). The basic concept of an infusion couldn't be more straightforward, and I guarantee you've already done it before. Ever made a cup of tea by pouring boiling water over a tea bag or tea leaves? Then you know how to make an infusion. This process is typically used in conjunction with delicate plant materials including leaves, flowers, and green stems, plus roots and aromatic seeds that have a high volatile oil content. Steeping these ingredients in (usually hot, but sometimes cold) water releases their flavors as well as their medicinal and nutritional properties. And the longer you steep the plant material, the more intense the infusion becomes. So, an infusion made simply for flavor might only be steeped for a few minutes, while one that's intended to be used as medicine will probably be steeped for much longer. (In both cases, though, it's important to cover the cup or pot to prevent the plant's precious essential oils from evaporating.)

Some plants possess mucilaginous, or slimy, properties that are more soluble in cold water. If that sounds unappetizing, consider this: that slipperiness moistens and soothes the mucous membranes and can be especially welcome on a hot, dry day or when you have a sore, irritated throat. Examples of these "demulcent" herbs include mallow and marshmallow roots, violet, borage, hibiscus, and chia seeds. To make a cold infusion, simply steep the plant material in cold water for a couple of hours or overnight.

Decoction is just a bit different. Tough, woody plant materials such as roots, barks, and non-aromatic seeds usually require a little extra heat to extract their flavors and healing properties. Instead of steeping them in hot or boiling water, it's best to simmer ingredients like these on the stove. The resulting tea—or decoction—is quite potent, in terms of both flavor and herbal health benefits.

In addition to infusions and decoctions, this chapter includes recipes for herb and fruit juices and "lemonades." That's because most of these drinks have one major ingredient in common: the use of water to coax out flavors, colors, and nutrients. Speaking of which, pay attention to the water you use in these recipes because it's an essential component that is often underestimated or overlooked. So, whether you use tap water, filtered water, or springwater, use clear, fresh water that tastes good on its own. (Avoid using distilled water: it tends to taste flat.)

Always make all of your teas, juices, and lemonades in nonreactive containers and pans; stay away from materials such as aluminum, which can react to acids and tannins in plant material. Don't worry, this won't limit your creativity. You can use a huge range of vessels for making infusions, from ceramic teapots to French presses to mugs topped with a small plate. Lots of people use mason jars, but that can be risky: if the glass is cold when boiling water is added, the jar might crack. If you use a glass jar for your infusions, warm it first by filling it with hot (but not boiling) water, and then discard the hot water after a minute or two.

These days, herbal teas and homemade juices and lemonades are just as delicious and restorative as they were in centuries past, and they're a great way to showcase the treasures you discover on your wildcrafting expeditions.

Common plants for infusions

Chamomile • Elderflower • Fennel seed • Ginger root • Holy basil • Nettle • Oat straw • Peppermint • Raspberry leaf • Red clover • Rosemary • Sage

Common plants for decoctions

Astragalus root • Burdock root • Birch bark • Dandelion root • Echinacea root • Ginger root Licorice root • Reishi mushroom • Sarsaparilla root • Wild cherry bark

Basic Infusion for Delicate Plant Material

HERE'S THE BASIC TEMPLATE FOR MAKING AN INFUSION, AND IT'S NOTHING if not flexible. You can halve the proportions to make a smaller batch or double them to make a larger one. Measuring plant material by weight is preferable to measuring it by volume, because volume can vary wildly depending on the size, shape, and cut of the plant material. That said, there's no need to rush out and buy a scale because you can make a fine infusion simply by measuring with your eyes, hands, and taste buds. All it takes is a little practice. If you don't have a scale, start with a couple of tablespoons of plant material and adjust as needed.

1 ounce (28 g) dried plant material or 2 ounces (56 g) fresh plant material
2 cups (470 ml) boiling water

Place the plant material in a heat-proof ceramic or glass container. Pour boiling water over the plant material and cover the container with a lid or a small plate. Let the infusion steep for 5 to 30 minutes (or even up to a day), depending on the desired strength and flavor of the tea. Strain through a fine-mesh strainer, pressing down on the plant material with a spoon to extract as much liquid as possible. Discard the solids. Use within 12 hours, or store in an airtight container, refrigerate, and use within 3 days. (If refrigerating, let the infusion cool to room temperature first.)

YIELD: ABOUT 1³/₄ CUPS (411 ML)

Decoction for Tough Plant Material

MAKING A DECOCTION IS AS SIMPLE AS MAKING AN INFUSION. AS WITH the Basic Infusion for Delicate Plant Material (page 24), feel free to halve or double the proportions to make a larger or smaller batch. When you're making your decoction, be sure to cut or break the plant material into small pieces; fresh roots and rhizomes, such as ginger root, may be thinly sliced or minced. If you don't have a scale, start with a couple of tablespoons of plant material and adjust as needed.

1 ounce (28 g) dried plant material or 2 ounces (56 g) fresh plant material
2 cups (470 ml) fresh, cold water

Place the plant material and water in a small saucepan. Cover and bring to a boil. Reduce the heat to low and simmer, covered, for 15 to 30 minutes or even longer, depending on the density of the plant material and the desired strength and flavor of the tea. Strain through a fine-mesh strainer, pressing down on the plant material with a spoon to extract as much liquid as possible. Discard the solids. Use within 12 hours, or store in an airtight container, refrigerate, and use within 3 days. (If refrigerating, let the decoction cool to room temperature first.)

YIELD: 1 TO 1³/₄ CUPS (235 TO 411 ML), DEPENDING ON SIMMERING TIME AND WATER CONTENT OF THE PLANT MATERIAL

Basic Juicing Methods for Fresh Fruit

There are a few ways to extract juice from fresh fruit, which is called for in some of the recipes in this book. Here's how:

- **Stove top:** Place your choice of chopped or lightly crushed fruit in a saucepan with just enough water to cover. Bring to a boil and skim off any foam with a large spoon. Lower the heat and simmer until the fruit is very soft, typically 15 to 25 minutes. Let cool and strain the juice through a fine-mesh strainer. Discard the solids (or taste them: if they have any flavor left, reserve them for another use).

- **Blender or food processor:** Puree the chopped or lightly crushed fruit in a blender or food processor. Strain the puree without squeezing through a jelly bag or nut milk bag to obtain a clear juice. Discard the solids.

- **Electric juicer:** Different juicers work differently, so always follow the manufacturer's instructions.

Peppermint-Fennel After-Dinner Tea

FENNEL AND MINT ARE BOTH RENOWNED FOR THEIR ABILITY TO RELAX the digestive muscles, allowing gas to move through the digestive system and relieving the cramping that can occur from eating too much or too fast, or from noshing on something that didn't quite agree with you. Here, I've amplified its effects (and flavor!) by adding a few other carminative, or gas-relieving, herbs.

1 teaspoon dried peppermint

1 teaspoon fennel seeds, lightly crushed

1 teaspoon dried lemon balm

½ teaspoon dried chamomile flowers

1 green cardamom pod, cracked (optional)

1 cup (235 ml) boiling water

Honey (optional)

Combine the peppermint, fennel seeds, lemon balm, chamomile, and cardamom in a heat-proof ceramic or glass container. Pour boiling water over and cover. Let steep for 10 minutes. Strain through a fine-mesh strainer; discard the solids. Sweeten with honey, if desired.

YIELD: 1 CUP (235 ML)

Botanical Note: Although peppermint (*Mentha x piperita*) is the most widely-recognized digestive aid, I've found that other species of wild and cultivated mint can be effective as well. These include water mint (*Mentha aquatica*) and spearmint (*Mentha spicata*). Consult your health care practitioner about using peppermint if you have gastroesophageal reflux disease (GERD).

WILD DRINKS AND COCKTAILS

Goldenrod Tea

NINETEENTH-CENTURY NATURALIST JOHN MUIR DESCRIBED GOLDENROD as "hopeful and strength-giving beyond any other flower that I know." If only his praise could save goldenrod from its undeserved bad reputation! People often assume that goldenrod causes seasonal allergies even though the culprit is usually ragweed, which also blooms in late summer and early fall. Ironically, herbal preparations of goldenrod can actually soothe hay fever symptoms such as itchy eyes and runny noses. With a taste reminiscent of green tea (and with up to seven times more antioxidants!), goldenrod makes a lovely tea, either hot or iced. This bright, happy blend is perfect for those days when you need a cup of sunshine.

1 tablespoon (1 g) dried goldenrod leaves and flowers
1 teaspoon dried spearmint
1 teaspoon dried lemon verbena
1 cup (235 ml) boiling water
Honey (optional)

Combine the goldenrod, spearmint, and lemon verbena in a heat-proof ceramic or glass container. Pour boiling water over and cover. Steep for 10 minutes. Strain through a fine-mesh strainer; discard the solids. Sweeten with honey, if desired. Serve hot or refrigerate for iced tea.

YIELD: 1 CUP (235 ML)

 Wildcrafting Tip: Although anise-scented goldenrod (*Solidago odora*) is particularly prized for tea, other species, such as *Solidago canadensis, Solidago gigantea*, and *Solidago virgaurea* may be used. (There are more than fifty species worldwide, so consult a field guide—and perhaps a local herbalist—to find out which species grow in your area.) To gather goldenrod, use pruning shears or your fingers to snip off the top portion of the stalk, including the flowers and a few of the uppermost leaves. Then strip off the leaves and flowers and dry them for tea. (To learn how to dry herbs, see page 14.)

Lavender Tea for Stress Relief

LAVENDER IS A GENTLY POWERFUL HERB, AND, FORTUNATELY, YOU DON'T need a lot of it to reap its benefits. In fact, too much can quickly overwhelm the nose and palate. That's why this stress-relieving tea has just enough lavender to soothe the senses without overpowering them. It also includes lemon balm (*Melissa officinalis*) and linden (*Tilia cordata*), two other herbs that are celebrated for their calming effects.

1 teaspoon dried lavender flowers

1 teaspoon dried lemon balm

1 teaspoon dried linden leaves and flowers

1 cup (235 ml) boiling water

Honey (optional)

Combine the lavender, lemon balm, and linden in a heat-proof ceramic or glass container. Pour boiling water over and cover. Steep for 10 minutes. Strain through a fine-mesh strainer; discard the solids. Sweeten with honey, if desired.

YIELD: 1 CUP (235 ML)

 Botanical Note: For culinary purposes like infusions, English lavender (*Lavandula angustifolia*) and French or Dutch lavender (*Lavandula x intermedia*) are preferable; other types can have unpleasant levels of camphor. Though not a true lavender, the lavender-scented *Hyptis emoryi*, or desert lavender, is lovely in teas, too.

Tulsi and Rose Petal Tea

THIS ELEGANT, ROSE-PETAL-SCENTED TEA TASTES LIKE A LIGHT BLACK tea, only it contains no true tea leaves—and no caffeine, either. Instead, its tea-like qualities come from raspberry leaves and tulsi, or holy basil. Raspberry leaves are just what they sound like, and they're gathered in spring, before the plant flowers and develops berries. Strongly tannic and blessed with high antioxidant levels, raspberry leaves make a great alternative to black tea. (Blackberry and strawberry leaves are also excellent substitutes for black tea.) Thanks to its powerful healing properties, tulsi has been revered in India for thousands of years and is considered to be an "adaptogen"; that is, it helps the body adapt to stress. Although you probably won't find it in the wild, it's worth growing in your garden or buying from an herb purveyor. I like the Krishna variety of holy basil (*Ocimum tenuiflorum*), which has purple-tinged leaves and a spicy taste.

2 teaspoons dried tulsi (holy basil) leaves

2 teaspoons dried rose petals

1 teaspoon dried raspberry leaves

2 green cardamom pods, cracked

1 cup (235 ml) boiling water

Honey (optional)

Combine the tulsi, rose petals, raspberry leaves, and cardamom pods in a heat-proof ceramic or glass container. Pour boiling water over and cover. Let steep for 5 minutes. Strain through a fine-mesh strainer; discard the solids. Sweeten with honey, if desired.

YIELD: 1 CUP (235 ML)

Variation: Tulsi and Rose Petal Tea can be transformed into a divine iced-tea smoothie. Just make the recipe as directed, but double the amount of herbs. Strain through a fine-mesh strainer; let cool, then add the tea to a blender with 3 frozen figs and honey to taste, and whizz until smooth.

Dandelion and Chicory Chai

FROM THEIR BRIGHT-YELLOW BLOSSOMS RIGHT DOWN TO THEIR ROOTS, dandelions (*Taraxacum officinale*) are incredibly nutritious. Earthy and slightly bitter in flavor, dandelion roots aid digestion and support liver health. For an extra layer of mocha-like richness, add a pinch of roasted chicory root (*Cichorium intybus*). The blue-flowered chicory is a relative of the dandelion.

½ cup (120 ml) water

2 thin slices fresh ginger

1 teaspoon coarsely ground roasted dandelion root

1 teaspoon coarsely ground roasted chicory root (or, if you haven't got it, an extra 1 teaspoon dandelion root)

2 black peppercorns, cracked

2 green cardamom pods, cracked

1 whole clove

1-inch (2.5 cm) piece of cinnamon stick, broken into pieces

½ cup (120 ml) milk of your choice

1 tablespoon (20 g) honey

Combine the water, ginger, dandelion root, chicory root, peppercorns, cardamom, clove, and cinnamon in a saucepan. Cover and bring to a boil. Reduce the heat to low and simmer, covered, for 5 minutes. Add the milk and honey; increase the heat to medium, and bring to a boil again, uncovered. Remove from the heat and strain into a cup. Discard the solids and serve immediately.

YIELD: 1 CUP (235 ML)

Wildcrafting Tip: Dig dandelion roots and then clean them by agitating them in water and scrubbing them with a brush. Chop the roots into small pieces and roast them in a dry cast-iron skillet, stirring continuously, until they're aromatic and a rich brown color. Let cool completely, and store in an airtight container. Grind them using a coffee grinder, spice grinder, or rolling pin. Chicory taproots can grow up to a couple of feet (61 cm), so digging them up is a more serious affair. Once you've cleaned them, thinly slice the roots and roast them for a couple hours in a low-temperature oven (about 200°F to 250°F, or 93°C to 121°C), and then store and grind as you would dandelion roots.

Berry Kompot

KOMPOT IS A JUICY, REFRESHING DRINK THAT HAILS FROM EASTERN Europe. It's traditionally made with whatever kind of fruit happens to be in season, and it's served chilled, with a bit of the fruit resting in the bottom of the glass. I'm especially enchanted by jewel-toned, sweet-and-tart kompots made from bramble berries such as blackberries, raspberries, and dewberries. Feel free to experiment with other berries, too. From currants and gooseberries to blueberries and mulberries, just about any kind of berry will work well.

1 pound (454 g) berries
1 quart (940 ml) water
¼ cup (50 g) sugar, or more to taste
Optional herbs: large sprig of lemon balm, mint, or rose geranium

Rinse and pick over the berries, discarding any stems or leaves. Bring the water to a boil in a large saucepan. Stir in the berries and sugar. Reduce the heat and simmer, uncovered, for 5 minutes. Remove from the heat, taste for sweetness, and add more sugar, if desired. If using herbs, add them to the pot now. Cover the pot and let the liquid cool to room temperature. Remove and discard any herbs. Strain the kompot through a fine-mesh strainer into an airtight container. If any whole berries remain, go ahead and add them to the juice: it makes for a nice presentation. (The crushed berry pulp that remains may be reserved for another use, such as a topping for oatmeal or yogurt.) Cover and refrigerate, and use within 1 week. Serve chilled.

YIELD: ABOUT 1 QUART (940 ML)

Sumac-ade

SUMAC SHRUBS POP UP ALL OVER THE WORLD. IN THE MIDDLE EAST, the plant's reddish berries (or, more accurately, drupes) are ground into a spice that lends a lemony flavor to salads, hummus, and other savory dishes. Using your trusty pruning shears, harvest clusters of sumac in the summer when the drupes are bright red or purple and taste nice and tart. (Sumac berries may also be dried in bunches and stored for later use.) Don't bother with sumac that has been recently rained on, because the flavor (and vitamin C) will have been washed away. Native Americans have used the entire sumac plant for food and medicine: the vitamin C-rich berries helped prevent scurvy during the long winter months.

2 handfuls packed sumac clusters

1 quart (940 ml) lukewarm (not hot) water

Simple Syrup (page 51), Honey Syrup (page 52), or maple syrup (optional)

Shake the sumac clusters to remove any dirt or insects. Don't rinse them: that'll wash away their trademark flavor. Cut off and discard any large stems, leaves, or green berries. Combine the sumac and water in a bowl or pitcher and lightly swish the berries around in the water using your hands or a wooden spoon. Let stand for about 2 hours, or until it tastes tart enough for you. Sumac berries are covered in small hairs that give them their tart flavor, but the hairs can irritate the mouth and throat when consumed in large amounts. Strain the liquid through a fine-mesh strainer lined with a coffee filter or muslin (straining removes these tiny hairs, and prevents them from irritating the mouth and throat). Discard the berries. If desired, sweeten with syrup. Serve chilled.

YIELD: 1 QUART (940 ML)

Botanical Note: There are many edible species of sumac (*Rhus* spp.), so consult a local field guide to find out which ones might grow in your area. Note that edible sumac is a completely different species from poison sumac (*Toxicodendron vernix*), which has white, not red, berries. Allergy sufferers take note: if you're sensitive to cashews or mangoes, you should avoid sumac, which is part of the same family.

Persimmon Punch

ALTHOUGH I LOVE GATHERING PINE NUTS IN THE WILD, I NEVER MANAGE to harvest very many. So, instead of burying them in a garlicky pesto, I like to use the nuts in a way that really highlights their unique shape and flavor. That's where this spiced Korean punch, called *sujeonggwa*, comes in. Redolent of cinnamon and ginger and garnished with pine nuts, it's often served chilled as a dessert or digestif, and is enjoyed on special occasions such as New Year's Day. Although this punch traditionally calls for dried Hachiya persimmons, you can also use dried wild American persimmons (*Diospyros virginiana*). Persimmons contain vitamin C and iron, and they're good sources of fiber, too. If you don't have a scale, start with ¼ cup (24 g) sliced ginger and adjust as needed.

2 ounces (56 g) peeled and thinly sliced ginger

4 (3-inch, or 7.5-cm) cinnamon sticks

2 quarts (1880 ml) water

½ cup brown sugar (115 g) or honey (170 g)

6 whole dried persimmons

1 tablespoon (9 g) pine nuts

Combine the ginger, cinnamon sticks, and water in a large saucepan. Cover and bring to a boil. Reduce the heat to low and simmer, covered, for 30 minutes. Strain through a fine-mesh strainer into a container; discard the solids. Stir in the sugar. Remove and discard the stems of the persimmons and add the persimmons to the liquid. Let cool to room temperature. Cover and refrigerate for at least 2 hours before serving. Serve chilled in a teacup or an Asian-style tea bowl with a persimmon in each cup. Garnish with the pine nuts.

YIELD: 6 SERVINGS

Hibiscus Cooler

TART, MAGENTA-COLORED HIBISCUS TEA IS MADE FROM THE CALYXES of the roselle flower (*Hibiscus sabdariffa*), which are a fine source of both vitamin C and antioxidants. World-renowned for its health benefits, hibiscus has a fruity, berry-like flavor and is known as *agua de Jamaica* in Latin America, *sorrel* in the Caribbean, *bissap* in West Africa, and *karkadé* in North Africa. Note that hibiscus can stain, so always use nonporous cookware and utensils when you're handling it—and be sure to take off your favorite white shirt before you start brewing.

½ cup (15 g) dried hibiscus flowers

1 quart (940 ml) cold water

¼ to ½ cup (60 to 120 ml) Simple Syrup (page 51)

Ice cubes

Lime slices, for garnish

Combine the hibiscus flowers and water in a large jar or pitcher. Cover and refrigerate for 8 hours or overnight. Strain through a fine-mesh strainer; discard the solids. Stir in the Simple Syrup to taste. Serve over ice and garnish with the lime.

YIELD: 1 QUART (940 ML)

Variation: Adding a few pinches of common mallow (*Malva neglecta*) or marshmallow (*Althaea officinalis*) leaves to the infusion will increase its cooling and soothing effects, particularly on the respiratory, digestive, and urinary systems. The tannins in the leaves will give the drink a flavor slightly more akin to iced tea. (Use the roots if you're after a thicker, more mucilaginous and medicinal brew.)

Wood Sorrel Lemonade

RICH IN VITAMIN C, WOOD SORREL IS ALSO KNOWN AS SOUR GRASS, DUE to the plant's tart, lemony flavor. The nineteenth-century English horticulturalist Maude Grieve describes a recipe in *Le Dictionnaire des Ménages* (1820), an early household management book, in a way that sums up Wood Sorrel Lemonade perfectly: it's "lemonade powder without lemons." This recipe is just as simple, and it's utterly delicious. I prefer it sans sweetener, but you can add Simple Syrup or Honey Syrup, if you like.

2 cups (60 g) packed wood sorrel (leaves, stems, flowers), chopped
2 cups (470 ml) boiling water
Simple Syrup (page 51) or Honey Syrup (page 52) (optional)

Place the wood sorrel in a nonreactive, heat-safe container. Pour the boiling water over the wood sorrel and give it a stir. Cover the container and let it steep for 15 minutes.

Strain the tea through a fine-mesh strainer without pressing on the plant material, then discard the solids. Let cool to room temperature. Cover and refrigerate. Serve over ice and sweeten with Simple Syrup or Honey Syrup, to taste, if desired.

YIELD: ABOUT 2 CUPS (470 ML)

Botanical Note: Wood sorrel (*Oxalis* spp.) is frequently mistaken for clover (*Trifolium* spp.), but it can be distinguished by its heart-shaped leaves. Look for wood sorrel in moist, shady areas, from forests to backyards. All wood sorrel species are edible, although some are more palatable than others. Sheep sorrel (*Rumex acetosella*) can also be used in this recipe. Both wood sorrel and sheep sorrel are high in oxalic acid; consult a health care practitioner if you are sensitive to oxalates or have kidney stones.

Cranberry Mors

MORS IS A TART, BERRY-BASED REFRESHER THAT HAS A HECK OF A PEDIGREE: it was first mentioned in the sixteenth-century Russian homemaking manual *Domostroy*. Though it's frequently made from cranberries, mors can easily be made with just about any kind of wild or cultivated sour berries. And, though modern-day mors is often sweetened with sugar, I prefer to use honey; it's a nod to the origin of the word *mors*, which probably derives from the Latin *mulsa*, or "honey drink." Forget about the store-bought stuff that comes in cartons: thanks to the natural pectin in the berries, this juice has a velvety texture.

2 cups (224 g) cranberries
5 cups (1175 ml) water
⅓ cup (113 g) honey, or more to taste
Juice of ½ lemon (about 1 tablespoon, or 15 ml)

Rinse and pick over the cranberries, discarding any stems or leaves. Combine the cranberries and water in a large saucepan. Bring to a boil and cook until the cranberries burst. Remove from the heat. Using a potato masher or the back of a large wooden spoon, thoroughly mash the cranberries in the pot. Return the pot to a boil and boil for 5 minutes. Remove from the heat. Stir in the honey and lemon juice. Cover and let cool to room temperature. Strain through a fine-mesh strainer into a container; discard the pulp, or, better yet, reserve it for another use. Cover and refrigerate, and use within 1 week. Serve chilled.

YIELD: ABOUT 1 QUART (940 ML)

Variation: Mors is wonderful as a hot drink, too. To make a spiced mulled drink, just simmer the strained mors with a cinnamon stick, a few strips of orange zest, and a couple of cloves for a few minutes over low heat, and serve immediately.

Variation: Try replacing the cranberries with another tart berry, such as red currants, gooseberries, lingonberries, barberries, highbush cranberries (*Viburnum trilobum*), or Cornelian cherries (*Cornus mas*).

Spring Greens Juice

NEXT TIME YOU'RE IN THE MOOD FOR A RESTORATIVE GREEN TONIC, don't head to your local juice bar: just poke around your backyard instead! Wild weeds such as dandelion greens (*Taraxacum officinale*) are highly nutritious and often abundant. Combine them with a few fruits and vegetables that are probably knocking around your fridge already, and your homemade tonic is done and dusted. To minimize their bitter flavor, pick dandelion greens when they're young, in early spring. (Or just embrace them and enjoy the bitterness!) Dandelion greens promote healthy digestion, and, as a diuretic, may even aid in lowering blood pressure.

1 cup (235 ml) water

Handful young dandelion greens

1 medium apple (5 ounces, or 140 g), cored and chopped

½ medium cucumber (4 ounces, or 112 g), peeled and chopped

Juice of ½ medium lemon (about 1 tablespoon, or 15 ml)

Honey to taste (optional)

Combine all the ingredients in a blender, and blend until smooth. You can strain out the pulp if you like, but I just leave it in for the extra fiber. Serve immediately in a tall glass.

YIELD: ABOUT 2 CUPS (470 ML)

Variation: Replace all or part of the dandelion greens with chickweed (*Stellaria media*), cleavers (*Galium aparine*), common mallow leaves (*Malva neglecta*), violet leaves and/or flowers (*Viola odorata* or *V. sororia*), or watercress (*Nasturtium officinale*).

Lemon Barley Water

A TRADITIONAL DRINK IN MANY COUNTRIES AROUND THE WORLD, including India and other parts of Southeast Asia, barley water is still produced commercially in England (where it's the official drink of Wimbledon). True, it's not an especially captivating name for a drink, but don't let that put you off. Barley water can offer serious refreshment on a hot summer day. Best served chilled, it tastes subtly nutty and not too sweet, making it a nice variation from regular lemonade.

½ cup (100 g) pearl barley

6 cups (1410 ml) water

Peel of 1 medium lemon, cut in wide strips

¼ cup (85 g) honey, or more to taste

Juice of 2 medium lemons (¼ cup, or 60 ml)

2 sprigs lemon balm or mint

Rinse the barley under cold water until the water runs clear. Drain well. Combine the barley, water, and lemon peel in a large saucepan. Cover and bring to a boil. Reduce the heat and simmer, covered, for 30 minutes. Strain through a fine-mesh strainer into a heat-proof container. Discard the lemon peel and reserve the barley for another use (toss it with vegetables and herbs to make a grain salad). Stir the honey into the hot barley water. Let cool to room temperature. Stir in the lemon juice and herbs. Cover and refrigerate in an airtight container. Serve chilled.

YIELD: ABOUT 1 QUART (940 ML)

Variation: The barley can be replaced with hulled Job's tears, a gluten-free grain that comes from a tall grass (*Coix lacryma-jobi*). Job's tears can be found in East Asian grocery stores; it also grows wild in parts of the northeastern and southern United States.

Rose Water

A STAPLE OF MIDDLE EASTERN CUISINE, ROSE WATER IS ALSO THE SECRET
ingredient in my sister-in-law Dana's lemonade. Making your own is easy, and the
rose water will last for ages in the fridge. Use the most fragrant roses you can find
(any species), and, as always, make sure they're pesticide-free. (If you use store-
bought roses, make sure they're intended for culinary use.) You don't need to
limit yourself to roses, either. This method can be applied to other fresh flowers or
herbs, such as orange blossoms or lavender. Use rose water to add a delicate floral
bouquet to lemonade, cocktails, sodas, and shrubs, such as the Raspberry Shrub
on page 100.

For this recipe, use a lidded saucepan with about a 12-quart (11.3 L) capacity
and a convex lid (a glass lid is ideal—that way, you'll be able to see what's going on
inside the pot). You'll also need two small and sturdy heat-safe bowls, such as rame-
kins or ceramic or glass cereal bowls: if you have one, a heat-safe glass measuring
cup works well for the second bowl.

6 cups (180 g) fresh rose petals

About 6 cups (1410 ml) water

Large resealable plastic bag filled with ice cubes,
 plus more ice cubes as needed

Gently shake the flowers to remove any dirt or insects. Place a small and sturdy heat-safe
bowl upside down in the center of a very large saucepan. Arrange the rose petals around
the sides of the bowl. Pour just enough water into the pot to cover the rose petals; the
water level should remain below the top of the bowl. Balance another bowl (right side up)
on top of the first bowl; this is what will catch your rose water. Cover the pot with the lid
flipped upside down.

Bring the water to a simmer over medium heat. Once it starts to simmer, put the bag of
ice on the inverted lid. Adjust the heat if necessary to maintain a gentle simmer. When
the ice cubes melt, pour out the water and add new ice cubes to the bag. As the steam rises
inside the pot, it will condense on the underside of the cold lid and drip into the open
bowl. Peek inside the pot occasionally; when you have about 1 cup (235 ml) of rose water
in the bowl (approximately $1^{1}/_{2}$ hours), turn off the heat. Let cool.

Uncover the pot and carefully lift out the bowl of rose water. Using a funnel, transfer the
rose water to a sterilized bottle. Store in the refrigerator for up to 6 months.

YIELD: ABOUT 1 CUP (235 ML)

SYRUPS, SQUASHES, AND CORDIALS

WELCOME TO THIS BOOK'S MOST VERSATILE CHAPTER! IT'S true: syrups, squashes, and cordials are mixological powerhouses that can work their magic on just about anything quaffable. A splash of syrup transforms a glass of plain fizzy water into a handcrafted soda and turns a basic cocktail recipe into your own signature drink. (You can even use syrups to flavor fermented drinks: see chapter 7 to find out how.) And syrups don't need to be confined to the glass, either. They can be used to great effect in cooking, transforming anything from vinaigrettes to a bowl of plain vanilla ice cream to roasted vegetables into a unique, memorable experience. What's more, they can capture the essence of a season, from the sweetness of wild strawberries in spring to the color of a cactus fruit in summer. Herbs, flowers, and even nuts can lend themselves to fine syrups, too, such as sweet, delicate honeysuckle or rich and milky hazelnuts.

Syrups boast a long and venerable history. The word *syrup* derives from the Arabic word *sharâb*, which can be loosely translated as "drink" or "beverage." Since medieval times, people in the Middle East have preserved herbs, flowers, spices, and fruit juices by simmering them with honey (and later, sugar) to form a thick, sweet concentrate with both therapeutic and culinary benefits. This nonalcoholic *sharâb* later became known as *sharbât* in Arabic and *sherbet* in Turkish. By the thirteenth century, *sharâb* had spread to Europe, becoming *sirop* in French and *syrup* in English. (Shrubs, featured in chapter 4, are also descended from the Middle Eastern *sharâb*.)

Traditionally, Middle Eastern syrups are made from fruits such as lemon, lime, pomegranate, and quince, as well as roots and spices such as ginger and cardamom. Mixed with water or ice, these syrups offer welcome refreshment in hot weather, and they're a pleasurable—and less dehydrating!—alternative to alcoholic drinks. As they spread to Europe and later America, syrups appealed to both apothecaries and cooks, who used them to make beverages and preserved fruits, and confections

such as sorbet (another word derived from *sharâb*). As time passed, syrup-makers were more likely to use sugar rather than honey, and often incorporated egg whites into the mix to help clarify the syrup (a technique that became unnecessary with the advent of modern sugar refining in the nineteenth century). In the nineteenth century, syrups became integral to the repertoire of the pharmacist, soda jerk, and bartender—professions that often overlapped with one another.

Squashes, in the context of drinks, are also close cousins of the *sharâb*. Forget those green and yellow gourds that pop up in the summer and autumn; *squash* is another common term for concentrated fruit syrups, and the name probably comes from the act of crushing or "squashing" fruit to make a sugar-sweetened syrup. Although squashes are typically diluted with still or carbonated water, they can also be used as cocktail mixers. Classic British squashes include lemon, orange, and blackcurrant, while in other parts of the world, such as India and Southeast Asia, you'll find squashes made from local fruits like mango, pineapple, and lychee.

Like squashes, cordials are concentrated,

nonalcoholic syrups made with fruit or herbs. (In the United States, a cordial is often synonymous with a liqueur, which is a strong, sweet alcoholic drink, but in the United Kingdom—and for the purposes of this book—cordials are traditionally booze-free.) The word *cordial* has its roots in the fourteenth century, when it originally referred to a medicinal drink or food that could invigorate the heart by stimulating blood circulation. *Cor* means "heart" in Latin, and even today, a "cor-dial" person is considered warmhearted, friendly, and gracious—exactly the qualities you might use to describe a person who shares his or her handmade drinks with friends and family.

Since their earliest days, syrups have been used for medicinal purposes as well as for refreshment. For instance, a six-teenth-century Mughal Indian painting depicts a physician with bottles labeled *sharbât*, presumably filled with medicinal syrups, and, even earlier, the Han dynasty text *Wushi'er Bingfang* (*Prescriptions for Fifty-Two Diseases*) documented nearly three dozen recipes for medicated syrups called *gao zi*. In ancient Greece, the physi-cian and botanist Dioscorides prescribed various syrups for ailments such as stomachaches and coughs. (Today, most of us are well familiar with cough syrup—even if the commercial versions have strayed from their herbal origins! Honey-based syrups are still particularly soothing to irritated mucous membranes, but even sugar-based syrups have these demulcent properties.) Finally, syrups have also been used to make bitter herbs more palatable: as Mary Poppins famously proclaimed, "a spoonful of sugar helps the medicine go down." Perhaps the

best syrups, then, are those that are both healthful and tasty, such as the immune-boosting Elderberry Rob on page 69. Read on to find out how easy it is to make your own.

Crafting Syrups and Squashes

MOST SYRUPS WILL LAST FOR A couple of weeks in the refrigerator, par-ticularly if they are stored in an airtight, sterilized container. (To find out how to sterilize your containers, see pages 18 and 19.) Adding a bit of vodka to your syrup can also extend its life span by two or three times without compromising its flavor. To do this, for each cup (235 ml) of syrup, stir in $1/4$ ounce ($1^1/2$ teaspoons, or 7 ml) of 100-proof vodka before refrigerating. Note that you should avoid using these syrups in drinks intended to be nonalcoholic.

For longer-term storage, syrups may also be frozen in freezer-safe containers, leaving at least 1 inch (2.5 cm) of head-space to allow for expansion. If you're freezing syrups in mason jars, be sure to use wide-mouth jars, because jars with necks are susceptible to cracking.

Many syrups can also be canned; how-ever, that is beyond the scope of this book. For guidance on safe canning practices, contact your state's university exten-sion office. (Check out the educational resources on page 183 for more.)

Basic Syrups

SYRUPS MAY BE USED TO SWEETEN COCKTAILS, LIQUEURS, AND OTHER drinks. Using these six recipes as bases; it's easy to customize syrups with interesting or in-season herbs, spices, and fruits. Rely on your taste buds as you move forward, because the ingredients you choose may release different flavors, depending on species, harvest season, and freshness. That's why it's helpful to think of these basic syrup recipes as handy guides. You may want to experiment with ingredient proportions and steeping times for infusions and decoctions. Also, using the basic one-to-one ratio of sugar to water, you can scale these recipes up to make syrups in larger volumes.

SIMPLE SYRUP

Made from equal parts sugar and water, this indispensable syrup may be used to sweeten alcoholic and nonalcoholic drinks including cocktails, liqueurs, teas, and lemonades.

1 cup (235 ml) water
1 cup (100 g) sugar

Combine the water and sugar in a small saucepan, and bring to a simmer over medium-low heat, stirring to dissolve the sugar. Simmer for another minute. Remove from the heat and let cool. Store in the refrigerator for up to 1 month, or up to 3 months with added vodka (see page 50).

YIELD: ABOUT 1 CUP (235 ML)

HONEY SYRUP

ALTHOUGH YOU COULD SIMPLY SWAP HONEY FOR THE SUGAR IN THE SIMPLE
Syrup (page 51) recipe, I prefer this method, because boiling raw honey can destroy its health benefits.

1 cup (235 ml) water
1 cup (340 g) honey

Warm the water in a small saucepan. Remove from the heat and stir in the honey until completely dissolved. Let cool. Store in the refrigerator for up to 1 month, or up to 2 months with added vodka (see page 50).

YIELD: ABOUT 1 CUP (235 ML)

SYRUP WITH HERBS, LEAVES, FLOWERS, OR AROMATIC SEEDS

FOLLOW THE SIMPLE SYRUP (PAGE 51) RECIPE, REPLACING THE WATER
with a strong infusion made by pouring hot or cold water over herbs, leaves, flowers, or seeds of your choice, letting them steep, and then straining out the solids. For detailed instructions, see the Basic Infusion recipe on page 24.

SYRUP WITH ROOTS, BARK, OR NON-AROMATIC SEEDS

FOLLOW THE SIMPLE SYRUP (PAGE 51) RECIPE, REPLACING THE WATER with a decoction made by simmering the roots, bark, or seeds in boiling water and then straining out the solids. For detailed instructions, see the Basic Decoction recipe on page 25.

SYRUP WITH FRUIT

FOLLOW THE SIMPLE SYRUP (PAGE 51) RECIPE, REPLACING THE WATER with fruit juice (see page 25 for detailed instructions). Fruit syrups will last in the refrigerator for 1 to 2 weeks, or up to a month with added vodka (see page 50).

BURNT SUGAR SYRUP

USE THIS SYRUP TO ADD A RICH, SLIGHTLY BITTER CARAMEL FLAVOR (and deep brown color) to cocktails, liqueurs, bitters, and fortified wines, such as the Sweet Vermouth on page 151.

½ cup (100 g) sugar
½ cup (120 ml) boiling water

Place the sugar in a heavy-bottomed saucepan with high sides. Cook over medium heat, without stirring, until the sugar melts. Once the sugar has melted, swirl the pan every 30 seconds and watch carefully as the sugar changes color. As soon as it turns deep amber in color and starts to smoke, remove the pan from the heat. Gradually pour the water into the pan, stirring constantly; the mixture will bubble vigorously. If the sugar seizes up, return the pan to low heat and cook, stirring constantly, until it returns to a syrupy consistency. Remove from the heat and let cool. Store in the refrigerator for up to 2 weeks, or up to a month with added vodka (see page 50).

YIELD: ¹/₂ CUP (120 ML)

Ginger Syrup

ALTHOUGH MOST OF US FIND GINGER IN THE GROCERY STORE RATHER than in our backyards, I couldn't resist including this recipe because it's so versatile and delicious. (Note that North American wild ginger, *Asarum canadense*, is a completely different plant so don't use it as a substitute here.) For best results, consume this zippy syrup within one week, and use it to add sweetness and warmth to sodas, cocktails, lemonades, and hot toddies. When made with honey, the syrup is a great addition to hot water with lemon, that dynamic duo: sip it to relieve ailments such as sore throats, nausea, and motion sickness.

¼ cup (1 ounce, or 28 g) peeled, thinly sliced fresh ginger
1¼ cups (295 ml) water
About 1 cup (200 g) sugar or ¾ cup (255 g) honey

Combine the ginger and water in a saucepan. Cover and bring to a boil. Reduce the heat to low and simmer, covered, for 30 minutes. Strain through a fine-mesh strainer; discard the ginger or reserve it for another use.

Measure the liquid; you should have about 1 cup (235 ml). Pour the liquid into a clean saucepan along with an equal volume of sugar (about 1 cup, or 200 g) or ³/₄ cup (255 g) honey. Bring to a simmer over medium-low heat, stirring to dissolve. Simmer for another minute. Remove from the heat and let cool. Store in the refrigerator for up to 2 weeks, but use within 1 week for best flavor.

YIELD: ABOUT 1 CUP (235 ML)

Kitchen Tip: To peel ginger safely and efficiently, skip the knives and vegetable peelers: instead, use the edge of a metal spoon to scrape the skin off the surface of the root.

Meyer Lemon and Bay Leaf Syrup

THIS SYRUP IS AN ODE TO MY ADOPTED STATE OF CALIFORNIA, HOME OF backyard Meyer lemon trees and wild bay leaves in abundance. I love pairing the sweet citrus with native California bay laurel leaves (*Umbellularia californica*) to make a syrup for dressing up sodas and gin cocktails. California bay leaves are more potent than—and some say inferior to—the Turkish bay leaves (*Laurus nobilis*) sold in most stores, but I actually prefer local leaves: perhaps that's because their scent reminds me of the time I spent gathering them in the woods.

½ cup (120 ml) Meyer lemon juice (from about 3 lemons)
1 cup (200 g) sugar
½ cup (120 ml) water
3 dried California bay leaves (or 6 dried Turkish bay leaves), torn in half
Peel of 1 Meyer lemon

Combine the lemon juice, sugar, and water in a small saucepan. Bring to a boil over medium heat, stirring to dissolve the sugar. Reduce the heat to low and simmer for 2 minutes. Remove from the heat. Stir the bay leaves and lemon peels into the pan. Let cool. Strain through a fine-mesh strainer; discard the solids. Store in the refrigerator for up to 2 weeks.

YIELD: ABOUT 1¼ CUPS (295 ML)

Variation: If you don't have Meyer lemons, you can use ¼ cup (60 ml) standard lemon juice and ¼ cup (60 ml) orange juice, and the peel from a standard lemon.

Apple and Mint Syrup

A SYRUP OF APPLES "FORTIFIES AND GLADDENS THE HEART," ACCORDING to the thirteenth-century *Anonymous Andalusian Cookbook*. And I won't argue with that! I'm not sure how chefs or apothecaries created apple syrups in the thirteenth century, but these days, this is how I make a delicately scented apple and herb version. It only calls for the peels of the apples, so it's a great use of scraps that might otherwise go to waste—for instance, when you make an apple pie. Be sure to use unwaxed, organically grown apples (red apples will give the syrup a pretty pink color). You can use any type of mint, including peppermint, spearmint, and apple mint.

½ cup (48 g) fresh mint leaves

Peels from 4 medium apples (about 1 cup, or 150 g)

1 cup (200 g) sugar

1 cup (235 ml) water

Place the mint leaves in a heat-proof bowl. Combine the apple peels, sugar, and water in a saucepan. Bring to a boil over medium heat. Reduce the heat and simmer, uncovered, for 5 minutes. Strain through a fine-mesh strainer into the bowl of mint leaves; discard the apple peels. Let cool to room temperature. Cover and refrigerate for 8 hours or overnight. Strain through a fine-mesh strainer; discard the mint. Store in the refrigerator for up to 2 weeks.

YIELD: ABOUT 1 CUP (235 ML)

Variation: Fresh chamomile flowers (*Matricaria chamomilla* or *Chamaemelum nobile*) or pineapple weed (*Matricaria discoidea*) also make good partners for apple's bright, sweet flavor. Simply replace the mint with ¼ cup (24 g) of either one. And, because steeping these herbs for too long can make the syrup taste bitter, steep them for 1 to 2 hours (or until it tastes good to you) instead.

Pink Peppercorn Syrup

WHENEVER I LEAD PLANT WALKS IN LOS ANGELES, PARTICIPANTS ARE astounded to discover that the little pink berries on ornamental trees planted in front yards, along roads, and throughout public parks are the same as the (rather pricey!) pink peppercorns you can buy in the store. Native to South America, pink peppercorns (*Schinus terebinthifolius, S. molle*) are not true peppercorns, but they have a pleasant spicy flavor alongside a fruitiness that makes this syrup delightful in cocktails. It's wonderful in cocktails that feature citrus, especially grapefruit (like the Pink Peppercorn Paloma, page 59, or a Grapefruit Collins), or red berries such as cranberries and strawberries. You can also drizzle a little bit of this syrup on citrus or berry salads or add it to fizzy water along with a dash of Rose Water (page 46) to make a deceptively complex, nonalcoholic soda.

1 cup (200 g) sugar

1 cup (235 ml) water

2 tablespoons (10 g) pink peppercorns, crushed

Combine the sugar and water in a saucepan. Bring to a simmer over medium-low heat, stirring to dissolve the sugar. Simmer for another minute. Remove from the heat and stir in the pink peppercorns. Refrigerate overnight. Strain through a fine-mesh strainer; discard the solids. Store in the refrigerator for up to 1 month.

YIELD: ABOUT 1 CUP (235 ML)

Botanical Note: Pink peppercorns are related to cashews, so if you suffer from tree nut allergies, it's best to avoid them. The plant's sap can also cause skin irritation in some people.

Pink Peppercorn Paloma

A FAVORITE LIBATION IN MEXICO, THE PALOMA (WHICH MEANS "DOVE" in Spanish) is a fizzy, refreshing cocktail, and I love to spice it up with a splash of Pink Peppercorn Syrup. Some paloma recipes call for grapefruit-flavored soda, but this one is a bit different. Because you're sweetening the drink with syrup, use plain club soda and fresh grapefruit juice instead. It's the perfect summertime drink, so skip the margaritas and mix up one of these kicked-up palomas instead.

Lime wedge

Kosher salt

½ ounce (15 ml) freshly squeezed lime juice

¾ ounce (23 ml) Pink Peppercorn Syrup (page 58)

2 ounces (60 ml) freshly squeezed white grapefruit juice

2 ounces (60 ml) tequila reposado

Ice cubes

Club soda, chilled

Grapefruit half-wheel and pink peppercorns, for garnish

Moisten the rim of a Collins or highball glass with a lime wedge and coat with the salt. Combine the lime juice, Pink Peppercorn Syrup, grapefruit juice, and tequila in a cocktail shaker. Add ice and shake well. Strain into the prepared glass. Add ice, top off with club soda, and stir. Garnish with the grapefruit and pink peppercorns.

YIELD: 1 SERVING

Variation: Stir some crushed pink peppercorn skins into the kosher salt before coating the rim of the glass.

Strawberry Squash

ARE WILD STRAWBERRIES ABUNDANT IN YOUR NECK OF THE WOODS? IF so, use your next batch to make this versatile Strawberry Squash. If not, a nice basket of farmers' market strawberries will do just fine. This syrup is delicious as is, but to add another dimension to it, steep herbs in it while it cools. Try a sprig of lemon verbena, lavender, rose geranium, or basil. Or change things up entirely and use this recipe with other sweet and juicy berries, such as mulberries, black-berries, or juneberries. Use this squash to make strawberry lemonade, sodas, or cocktails such as a strawberry mojito, strawberry bourbon smash, or a Champagne cocktail. You can even drizzle it on waffles or ice cream sundaes!

1 tablespoon (15 ml) freshly squeezed lemon juice
1 cup (235 ml) water
1 cup (200 g) sugar
¾ pound (340 g) strawberries, hulled and quartered

Combine the lemon juice, water, and sugar in a saucepan. Bring to a boil over medium heat, stirring to dissolve the sugar. Stir in the strawberries. Reduce the heat and simmer gently, stirring occasionally, for 20 minutes. Remove from the heat and let cool. Strain through a fine-mesh strainer, gently pressing on the strawberries to extract the liquid without forcing the pulp through the strainer. Discard the solids. Store in the refrigerator for up to 2 weeks.

YIELD: ABOUT 2 CUPS (470 ML)

Pine Syrup

NEVER NIBBLED ON A PINE NEEDLE, FIR TIP, OR SPRUCE LEAF? TRY IT!
Chances are you'll be rewarded with lemon, orange, or other citrus flavors, and you'll also be getting a healthy dose of vitamin C. This recipe starts out as a strong tea—tasty and healing in itself—and ends with a syrup that you can use to perk up a glass of fizzy water, a mug of hot tea, or a cocktail (such as the Rye and Pine Old-Fashioned on page 63). Plus, teas and syrups made from these conifers have decongestant and expectorant effects that can be helpful during the winter cold and flu season. This syrup works well with other conifers like spruce, fir, or Douglas fir. Flavors vary between seasons (and even individual plants), so nibble as you forage and pick what tastes and smells good to you.

1 small handful conifer tips or needles, roughly chopped

1 cup (235 ml) boiling water

1 cup (200 g) sugar

Place the conifer tips or needles in a heat-proof ceramic or glass container. Pour boiling water over and cover the container. Let steep for at least 30 minutes and up to 24 hours. Strain through a fine-mesh strainer into a saucepan; discard the solids. Add the sugar to the pan. Bring to a simmer over medium-low heat, stirring to dissolve the sugar. Simmer for another minute. Remove from the heat and let cool. Store in the refrigerator for up to 1 month.

YIELD: ABOUT 1 CUP (235 ML)

Wildcrafting Tip: Harvest pine (*Pinus* spp.), fir (*Abies* spp.), Douglas fir (*Pseudotsuga menziesii*), or spruce (*Picea* spp.) needles from the new growth at the tips of branches. In spring, you can often pinch the tender, bright green tips with your fingers; later in the season, use pruning shears to clip a few inches off the ends. Move around, and make sure not to harvest too much from any single tree. Also, never cut the top of a tree: that can make it vulnerable to decay and disease.

Rye and Pine Old-Fashioned

JUST BECAUSE A COCKTAIL'S CALLED AN OLD-FASHIONED DOESN'T MEAN you can't experiment with it. This recipe replaces the standard sugar or simple syrup with Pine Syrup, which is a beautiful complement to robust rye whiskey. The result is a cocktail that's spicy and aromatic.

½ ounce (15 ml) Pine Syrup (page 62), or to taste

2 dashes aromatic bitters

2 ounces (60 ml) rye whiskey

Ice cubes

Lemon or orange twist

Combine the Pine Syrup and aromatic bitters in an old-fashioned glass. Add the whiskey and stir. Fill the glass with ice and stir again. Garnish with a twist of lemon, and serve immediately.

YIELD: 1 SERVING

Rose Hip Syrup

ROSE HIPS ARE THE BERRY-LIKE FRUITS THAT DEVELOP AFTER ROSES drop their petals. They're so high in vitamin C that when Britain was experiencing citrus shortages during World War II, the ministry of health sent volunteers out to the hedgerows to gather valuable rose hips for syrup making. (Vitamin C is essential to a healthy diet: it prevents diseases like scurvy, may boost the efficiency of the immune system, and is important for the growth and repair of tissues, including bones and skin.) Rose hips are tastiest after a frost, which sweetens their flavor. To process them, cut the hips in half, remove the hairy seeds, and dry the skins for year-round use in teas, syrups, elixirs, compotes, and jellies.

2 cups (400 g) fresh rose hips
2 cups (470 ml) water
1 cup honey (340 g) or sugar (200 g)

Rinse the rose hips to remove dirt, and trim away any stems or leaves (it's okay to leave the tops on). Lightly crush the rose hips using a potato masher or rolling pin. Combine the rose hips and water in a saucepan. Cover and bring to a boil. Reduce the heat to low and simmer, covered, for 20 minutes. Remove from the heat and crush the rose hips with a potato masher or another mashing tool. Strain through a fine-mesh strainer; discard the solids. Measure the liquid; you should have about 1 cup (235 ml). Return the liquid to the saucepan and add an equal volume of honey or sugar (about 1 cup [340 or 200 g]). Simmer for 5 minutes. Remove from the heat and let cool completely. Strain through a cloth or coffee filter to catch any little hairs, which can irritate the digestive system. Store in the refrigerator for up to 2 weeks.

YIELD: ABOUT 1 CUP (235 ML)

Variation: Whole dried rose hips can be substituted for fresh ones: use 1¼ cups (100 g) instead. They're usually too hard to crush by hand in the same way as fresh rose hips, but a food processor or mortar and pestle can do the job well. To substitute dried rose hips that have already been cut and sifted, use ¾ cup (60 g) instead of 1¼ cups (100 g).

Rose Hip Whiskey Smash

IT'S A DISTANT COUSIN OF THE MINT JULEP, BUT TAKE MY WORD FOR IT:
this Rose Hip Whiskey Smash is so much more exciting. Because the combination
of rose hip and mint is one of my favorites when it comes to tea, I decided to put
them side by side in a cocktail, too. And I'm glad I did, because pairing them with
bourbon and orange is pure magic. You'll get the best results if you use blood
orange, which brings a rosy color to the drink, plus a subtle berry flavor that's a nice
match for the rose hips.

3 orange wedges (preferably blood orange)

1 ounce (30 ml) Rose Hip Syrup (page 64)

4 to 6 fresh mint leaves

2 ounces (60 ml) bourbon

Ice cubes

Fresh mint sprig, for garnish

Muddle the orange wedges with the Rose Hip Syrup in the bottom of a cocktail shaker.
Add the mint leaves and lightly bruise with the muddler. Add the bourbon and ice and
shake well. Strain into an old-fashioned glass filled with crushed ice. Garnish with the
mint sprig.

YIELD: 1 SERVING

Citrus Squash

I LIKE TO USE A MIX OF ORANGE, GRAPEFRUIT, LEMON, AND MANDARIN orange, but you can use whatever you happen to have on hand. Flavoring this syrup with citrus peels gives it a more complex and concentrated flavor than you'd get from plain juice. (As with all recipes that include citrus peels, be sure to use unwaxed fruit that's free from pesticides.) I like to share a carafe of this sunny citrus squash at brunch gatherings, so that guests can fix their own drinks: some folks use it to make a vibrant juice with cold water, while others prefer a mimosa made with bubbly Prosecco.

1¼ pounds (568 g) citrus fruit
1 cup (235 ml) water
1 cup (200 g) sugar

Using a vegetable peeler, peel the citrus rind into wide strips, taking care to avoid the bitter white pith. Combine the citrus peels, water, and sugar in a medium saucepan. Bring to a boil over low heat, stirring to dissolve the sugar. Remove from the heat. Squeeze the juice from the citrus and strain to remove excess pulp and seeds. Measure the juice; you should have about 1 cup (235 ml). If you have significantly less than 1 cup (235 ml), top it off with more juice or water. If you have significantly more than 1 cup (235 ml), drink the surplus or save it for another use.

Add the 1 cup (235 ml) of juice to the saucepan, and bring to a boil. Remove from the heat immediately and let cool to room temperature. Strain through a fine-mesh strainer; discard the peels or reserve them for another use. Refrigerate for up to 2 weeks.

YIELD: ABOUT 2¹/₂ CUPS (590 ML)

> **Kitchen Tip:** You can use the leftover peels to make candied citrus peels. To do this, spread the peels on a wire rack and let them dry for 30 minutes. Roll the peels in sugar and dry them on a clean wire rack until no longer sticky (about 24 hours, or longer in humid climates). Store in an airtight container for up to 1 week, or in the freezer for up to a couple of months. These may be less tender than traditional candied citrus, but they can still be chopped up and used in baked goods, in granola, or on top of ice cream.

Elderflower Cordial

I FELL HEAD OVER HEELS IN LOVE WITH ELDERFLOWER CORDIAL WHEN
I lived in England. Later, I was delighted to discover that elder trees or shrubs grow
in many parts of the world—even near my home in urban Los Angeles. Since then,
every summer I make and freeze big batches of this sunny, Muscat-flavored syrup to
enjoy throughout the year. The classic version is sweetened with sugar, and it tastes
fine—but when I switched to honey, which I use in this recipe, my elderflower cordial
got more compliments than ever. To serve elderflower cordial, dilute it with still or
sparkling water, or add it to a glass of Prosecco or a gin and tonic for extra sparkle.
In addition to elderflowers (*Sambucus nigra, S. nigra* ssp. *canadensis, S. nigra* ssp.
cerulea), this method of syrup-making can be used with other flowers such as
meadowsweet (*Filipendula ulmaria*) and manzanita (*Arctostaphylos* spp.).

12 to 15 elderflower heads, depending on size (or 1 ounce [28 g] dried flowers)
1 medium lemon, thinly sliced
3 cups (705 ml) water
2 cups (680 g) honey

Gently shake the elderflower heads to remove any dirt or insects. Separate the flowers
from the stems, trying to remove as many of the stems as you can (a few are fine, but
too many can make you sick because they contain cyanide-inducing glycosides). Place
the flowers in a large, heat-proof bowl along with the lemon slices. Warm the water in a
medium saucepan. Remove from the heat and stir in the honey. Pour the mixture over the
elderflowers and lemon slices. Cover the bowl with a clean dish towel and let stand for 1 to
2 days, sampling every so often until the flavor is strong enough for you. Strain through a
fine-mesh strainer; discard the solids. Store in the refrigerator for up to 2 weeks. This cordial also freezes well. To freeze, pour into freezer-safe containers, leaving 1 inch (2.5 cm)
of headspace to allow for expansion.

YIELD: ABOUT 5 CUPS (1175 ML)

Variation: To use sugar instead of honey, replace the honey with 4 cups (800 g) sugar. Boil
the sugar with 1 quart (940 ml) water to make Simple Syrup (page 51). Let cool slightly, and
proceed as above.

Elderberry Rob

ALTHOUGH IT SOUNDS PRETTY EXOTIC, A "ROB" IS JUST A SEVENTEENTH-century name for a syrup. Robs were sometimes made with added sugar, or simply by boiling down fruit or vegetable juice until it thickens. In England, elderberry rob often included spices such as cinnamon, ginger, and cloves, but in this recipe, they're optional: that way, you get to decide whether you'd like a pure elderberry syrup or a spiced one. Elderberries (*Sambucus nigra, S. nigra* ssp. *canadensis, S. nigra* ssp. *cerulea*) are high in vitamin C, and elderberry extract has been shown to shorten the duration of a flu by about three days. This syrup can be taken as an immune booster during cold and flu season, but it can also be enjoyed year-round for its rich, grape-like flavor.

1 cup (150 g) fresh elderberries or ½ cup (75 g) dried

1½ cups (355 ml) water

1-inch (2.5 cm) piece fresh ginger root (optional)

1 cinnamon stick (optional)

4 cloves (optional)

½ cup honey (170 g) or 1 cup sugar (200 g)

Combine the elderberries, water, ginger, and spices in a medium saucepan. Bring to a boil, crushing the berries with a potato masher or the back of a large spoon. Reduce the heat to low and simmer for 20 minutes. Remove from the heat and crush the berries to release more juice. Strain through a fine-mesh strainer; discard the solids. If using honey, stir the honey into the warm juice. If using sugar, combine the juice and sugar in a saucepan. Bring to a boil, stirring to dissolve the sugar. Simmer for another minute and then remove from the heat. Let cool. Store in the refrigerator for up to 1 month.

YIELD: ABOUT 1 CUP (235 ML)

Hazelnut Orgeat

PRIMARILY USED IN MAI TAI COCKTAILS, ORGEAT (PRONOUNCED or-ZHA) has plenty of other uses. It can be mixed with sparkling water to make a homemade soda, and it's a good sweetener for lemonade, hot tea, and coffee. The result is a milky, delicately nutty syrup. My version calls for hazelnuts, but you can use any nuts you like, including hickory nuts, pecans, and walnuts. Blanched or peeled nuts are ideal, but if it feels like too much work, just leave the skins on.

2 cups (8 ounces, or 224 g) blanched hazelnuts (also known as filberts)
2 cups (470 ml) water
2 cups (400 g) sugar
Dash orange flower water (optional)

Place the hazelnuts and water in a blender or food processor. Pulse until the hazelnuts are finely chopped but not pureed. Pour the hazelnuts and water into a bowl. (To chop without a food processor, crush the hazelnuts with a rolling pin and then stir them into the water.) Cover the bowl and let stand for 8 hours or overnight.

Line a fine-mesh strainer with a fine-mesh bag or flour sack cloth and strain the liquid into a saucepan. Squeeze the bag or cloth to extract as much liquid as possible. Discard the hazelnut pulp. Stir the sugar into the hazelnut liquid. Warm the mixture over low heat (but do not boil), stirring until the sugar is dissolved. Remove from the heat and let cool. Stir in the orange flower water. Store in the refrigerator for up to 2 weeks. (Because this is an oil and water emulsion, the orgeat will separate in the refrigerator, so always shake well before using.)

YIELD: ABOUT 2¹/₂ CUPS (590 ML)

How to Blanch Hazelnuts. The following instructions are for 2 cups (224 g) of hazelnuts. Bring 5 cups (1175 ml) of water to a boil in a deep saucepan. Add ¼ cup (55 g) of baking soda and the hazelnuts to the pot. The water will foam up and turn purplish black; be ready with a large spoon and a bowl to skim off any foam that threatens to boil over. Boil the hazelnuts for 3 minutes. Test a hazelnut by rinsing it under cold water; the skin should slip off easily. If the skin clings, boil the hazelnuts a little longer. Drain the hazelnuts and plunge them into a bowl of cold water. Using your hands, rub the skins off the hazelnuts. When you've finished peeling all the hazelnuts, give them another rinse and drain. (Method adapted from Rose Levy Beranbaum, *The Cake Bible* [William Morrow, 1988].)

La Noisette Verte

SILKY ORGEAT SYRUP—LIKE MY HAZELNUT ORGEAT ON PAGE 70—AND anise-flavored spirits are a time-honored pairing. They make appearances in French aperitifs such as the Mauresque and Momisette, as well as the classic gin-and-absinthe cocktail called Gaby des Lys. So, in that grand tradition, here's my take on an orgeat and absinthe cocktail. La Noisette Verte (or the "the green hazelnut") makes an excellent happy-hour or pre-dinner drink.

¾ ounce (23 ml) Hazelnut Orgeat (page 70)

¾ ounce (23 ml) freshly squeezed lemon juice

2 ounces (60 ml) dry gin

3 dashes absinthe

Ice cubes

Combine the Hazelnut Orgeat, lemon juice, gin, and absinthe in a cocktail shaker. Add ice and shake well. Strain into a chilled cocktail glass.

YIELD: 1 SERVING

Hawthorn Cordial

THE WORD "CORDIAL" COMES FROM THE MEDIEVAL LATIN TERM *CORDIALIS*, meaning "of the heart," and hawthorn (*Crataegus monogyna, C. laevigata*) has been used for thousands of years in Asia and Europe to protect and strengthen the physical and emotional heart, improving blood circulation, and healing anxiety and sadness. So, how could I resist making a cordial that literally warms the heart? Hawthorn's red berries, or haws, are gently sweet and sour with an appley sort of flavor. I like to warm up my Hawthorn Cordial with a little ginger, which complements the haws' flavor and improves blood circulation to boot.

2 cups (400 g) fresh hawthorn berries (or 1 cup [120 g] dried)

1-inch (2.5 cm) piece fresh ginger, peeled and thinly-sliced

3 cups (705 ml) water

1 cup (340 g) honey or (200 g) sugar

Combine the hawthorn berries, ginger, and water in a saucepan. Bring to a boil. Reduce the heat to low and simmer, uncovered, for 10 minutes. Lightly crush the berries with a potato masher or another mashing tool, and continue simmering for another 10 minutes. Strain through a fine-mesh strainer and discard the solids. Measure the liquid; you should have about 1 cup (235 ml). Return the liquid to the saucepan and add the honey or sugar. Simmer for 5 minutes. Remove from heat and let cool completely. Store in the refrigerator for up to 2 weeks.

ABOUT 1 CUP (235 ML)

Variation: Replace the hawthorn with vitamin A- and C-rich American mountain ash or rowan berries (*Sorbus americana, S. alnifolia*).

Honeysuckle Syrup

HONEYSUCKLE, ALSO KNOWN AS WOODBINE (*LONICERA JAPONICA*), SPORTS sweetly scented flowers that aren't just pretty: they're also powerfully antiviral and antibacterial. Used in China for centuries to help fight colds and flu, the flowers can soothe an inflamed sore throat and cool down an overheated body on a scorching summer day. Try adding a splash of this delicately flavored syrup to lemonade, fizzy water, Champagne, or hot tea, or drizzle it on fresh berries. (I recommend using sugar, not honey, in this recipe, because honey can overwhelm honeysuckle's flavor. If you do want to try it, though, choose a mild varietal, such as a light clover honey or your local wildflower honey.)

1 cup (20 g) fresh honeysuckle flowers or ½ cup (10 g) dried
1¼ cups (295 ml) water
About 1 cup (200 g) sugar

Gently shake the honeysuckle flowers to remove any dirt or insects. Separate the flowers from the stems and discard any leaves and berries, which can be poisonous in large amounts. Place the flowers in a heat-proof ceramic or glass container. Bring the water to a boil. Pour it over the flowers and cover the container. Let the mixture stand at room temperature for 12 to 24 hours. Strain through a fine-mesh strainer; discard the solids.

Measure the liquid; you should have about 1 cup (235 ml). Combine the liquid and an equal volume of sugar (about 1 cup, or 200 g) in a saucepan. Bring to a simmer over medium-low heat, stirring to dissolve the sugar. Simmer for another minute. Remove from the heat and let cool. Store in the refrigerator for up to 2 weeks.

YIELD: ABOUT 1 CUP (235 ML)

Variation: This recipe also works well with fresh nasturtium flowers (*Tropaeolum majus*): the result is a golden, peppery syrup.

Honeysuckle Blackberry Cocktail

IF YOU'RE USING HONEYSUCKLE SYRUP IN COCKTAILS, YOU WANT TO highlight its delicate floral flavor, not overpower it. That's why mixing it with vodka works so well: it's a clean, neutral spirit. Honeysuckle flowers typically bloom between spring and summer, so I like to enhance this drink with fresh, seasonal ingredients, like succulent blackberries. Muddle a few berries in your cocktail shaker and they'll infuse the drink with sweet, tart flavors, plus a shot of color (and maybe a few antioxidants to boot). *Voilà*: an easy, refreshing drink that's perfect for brunches, garden parties, or summery afternoon gatherings.

4 blackberries

¾ ounce (23 ml) Honeysuckle Syrup (page 74)

¾ ounce (23 ml) freshly squeezed lemon juice

2 ounces (60 ml) vodka

Ice cubes

Honeysuckle flowers or mint sprig, for garnish

Muddle the blackberries with the Honeysuckle Syrup and lemon juice in the bottom of a cocktail shaker. Add the vodka and ice and shake well. Pour into a cocktail glass without straining. Garnish with the honeysuckle flowers.

YIELD: 1 SERVING

Prickly Pear Squash

ONE OF MY FAVORITE THINGS ABOUT SUMMER IS THE WAY RIPE PRICKLY pear cactus (*Opuntia* spp.) fruits brighten Southern California's dry landscape with splashes of magenta, tangerine, and gold. Prickly pear fruits, or *tunas*, are also anti-inflammatory, cooling, and moistening—exactly the qualities you're looking for in a refreshing tipple. With more than 100 species, prickly pear cacti vary widely in flavor: some are reminiscent of bubblegum while others evoke watermelon, persimmon, and kiwi. Native to the Americas, they now grow worldwide.

2 pounds (908 g) prickly pear fruits (about 12 large)
1 cup (200 g) sugar
1 tablespoon (15 ml) freshly squeezed lemon juice (from about ½ lemon)

Carefully remove the glochids or spines from the prickly pear fruits by scraping them off with a sharp knife or burning them off with a torch or an open flame. (If you are using store-bought fruits, the spines may have already been removed.) Cut each fruit in half lengthwise and scoop out the flesh with a spoon. Roughly chop the flesh and place it in a medium saucepan with just enough water to cover. Bring to a boil, lightly mashing the fruit with a wooden spoon. Reduce the heat to low and simmer until the fruit is very soft, about 20 minutes. Strain through a fine-mesh strainer; discard the solids.

Measure the juice; you should have about 1 cup (235 ml). Combine the juice, an equal volume of sugar (about 1 cup, or 200 g), and the lemon juice in a small saucepan. Bring to a simmer over medium-low heat, stirring to dissolve the sugar. Simmer for another minute. Remove from the heat and let cool. Store in the refrigerator for up to 2 weeks.

YIELD: ABOUT 1 CUP (235 ML)

Prickly Pear Ginger Beer Margarita

THE SYRUP ADDS VIBRANT COLOR AND FRUITY SWEETNESS TO THIS tequila-based cocktail. It's great with Mexican cuisine, or on its own as a refreshing afternoon thirst-quencher.

2 ounces (60 ml) silver tequila

1 ounce (30 ml) freshly squeezed lime juice

1 ounce (30 ml) Prickly Pear Squash (page 76)

Ice cubes

3 ounces (90 ml) chilled ginger beer (or Ginger Ale, page 164)

Lime wedge, for garnish

Combine the tequila, lime juice, and Prickly Pear Squash in a cocktail shaker. Add ice and shake well. Strain into an ice-filled glass. Top with the ginger beer. Stir and garnish with a lime wedge.

YIELD: 1 SERVING

Rhubarb and Rose Syrup

THIS SYRUP RECIPE CALLS FOR GOOD OLD CULTIVATED RHUBARB, the kind you'd find in your garden or at the farmers' market. The pink or red color of the stems turns this syrup a glorious shade of pink, which is echoed in the accompanying flavor of rose. Native to Central Asia, rhubarb has been used medicinally for thousands of years by the Chinese, Arabs, Greeks, and Romans, and the root was an important trade product mentioned in texts by explorers such as Marco Polo. But it wasn't until the eighteenth century that common garden rhubarb (*Rheum rhabarbarum*) was cultivated in England for its stems, and treated like a fruit in recipes for pastries and preserves. Pies aren't the only use for rhubarb stems, either: a tart rhubarb syrup such as this one can enhance soda water, sparkling wine, a gin-based cocktail, or even a slice of sponge cake. If the invasive Japanese knotweed (*Fallopia japonica*) grows in your area, you can also experiment with the shoots as a substitute for rhubarb.

8 ounces (224 g) rhubarb stalks, diced (about 1½ cups, or 224 g)

1 cup (200 g) sugar

1 cup (235 ml) water

1 cup (30 g) firmly packed fresh rose petals or ½ cup (6 g) dried

Combine the rhubarb, sugar, and water in a medium saucepan. Bring to a boil over medium heat, stirring to dissolve the sugar. Cover the pan, reduce the heat to low, and simmer until the rhubarb is falling apart and the color has leached into the water, about 15 minutes. Remove from the heat and stir in the rose petals. Let cool completely. Strain through a fine-mesh strainer, gently pressing on the rhubarb to extract the liquid. Discard the pulp or save it for another use (although it will be a bit chewy from the rose petals, it makes a delicious jam for toast). Store in the refrigerator for up to 2 weeks.

YIELD: ABOUT 1¼ CUPS (295 ML)

Variation: Instead of using the rose petals, stir ¼ teaspoon or more Rose Water (page 46) into the syrup after straining out the rhubarb.

Rhubarb and Rose Sour

DELIGHTFULLY PINK, FROTHY, AND CHEERFUL, THIS DRINK IS BEST
when it's made with a lighter, more floral gin, such as the homemade Summer
Gin on page 114, or a distilled gin like Hendrick's. My Rhubarb and Rose Syrup
heightens the tart and floral notes here, while the egg white adds a silky texture,
plus voluptuous quantities of foam. I like to make this Rhubarb and Rose Sour
with very fresh, pasture-raised eggs from a local chicken farmer, but you could
also use pasteurized egg whites, if you prefer.

½ ounce (15 ml) freshly squeezed lemon juice

1 ounce (30 ml) Rhubarb and Rose Syrup (page 78)

2 ounces (60 ml) gin

1 egg white (¾ ounce, or 23 ml) (pasteurized if you wish)

Combine the lemon juice, Rhubarb and Rose Syrup, gin, and egg white in a cocktail shaker.
Shake vigorously until frothy, about 1 minute. Fill the shaker with cracked ice and shake
until chilled. Double-strain into a coupe glass.

Variation: To turn this cocktail into a fizz, double-strain it into a fizz or highball glass, then top
with chilled club soda and stir gently.

Quince Sharbât

ONE OF MY FAVORITE PASTIMES IS HUNTING FOR FRUIT IN ABANDONED or empty lots. I usually find citrus trees, so you can imagine the thrill I got when I discovered a quince! If you don't have quince trees nearby, never fear. Seek them out in the fall at farmers' markets or Middle Eastern grocery stores. When they're cooked, the dry, knobby-looking fruits turn succulent and jammy, and their juices can be made into a fragrant, rosy syrup—or *sharbât*, as it's known in Iran. Serve this Quince Sharbât ice-cold, diluted with still or sparkling water, or dilute it with hot water to make a "tea"; the natural pectin in the quince can help soothe a dry, scratchy throat. When it comes to mixology, Quince Sharbât can also work in cocktails with a wide variety of spirits, such as gin, whiskey, brandy, and vodka.

2 tablespoons (30 ml) freshly squeezed lemon juice

2 cups (470 ml) water

1 pound (454 g) quince

½ cup (170 g) honey

½ cup (100 g) sugar

3 green cardamom pods, cracked

⅛ teaspoon rose water, homemade (page 46) or store-bought (optional)

Combine the lemon juice and water in a medium saucepan. Quarter each quince and remove and discard the core. Cut the quince into ½-inch (1.3 cm) chunks, dropping the chunks into the lemon water as you go along to prevent them from discoloring.

Add the honey, sugar, and cardamom pods to the pan. Bring to a boil over medium heat, stirring to dissolve the honey and sugar. Reduce the heat to low and simmer, covered, until the quince is very soft, about 45 minutes. Strain through a fine-mesh strainer. Reserve the cooked fruit for another use (it's delicious on everything from oatmeal to ice cream!). Let the syrup cool completely. Stir in the rose water. Store in the refrigerator for up to 2 weeks.

YIELD: ABOUT 2½ CUPS (590 ML)

Date Syrup

THIS RECIPE WAS INSPIRED BY THE *JALLAB* SYRUPS—TYPICALLY MADE from date syrup, grape molasses, rose water, and incense—that are served at some of my favorite Lebanese restaurants. The dried fruits are so sweet on their own that you don't need to add any sugar: in fact, this Date Syrup makes a great natural sweetener for all kinds of food and drink. Use it in place of honey, maple syrup, or molasses. I like adding this potassium- and iron-rich syrup to smoothies, milk, hot cocoa, yogurt, and marinades.

1½ cups (12 ounces, or 340 g) packed pitted dates
½ cup (3 ounces, or 84 g) packed dark raisins
3 cups (705 ml) water

Combine the dates, raisins, and water in a medium saucepan. Bring to a simmer over medium heat. Cover, reduce the heat, and simmer for 45 minutes. Remove from the heat. Line a strainer with a fine-mesh bag or cloth and set it over a bowl. Pour the contents of the pan into the strainer and let it stand until the fruit is cool enough to handle. Gather the bag or cloth around the fruit and squeeze to extract all the liquid. Reserve the pulp for another use.

Pour the liquid into a clean saucepan. Bring to a simmer, uncovered, over medium-low heat. Cook at a gentle, steady simmer, stirring occasionally, until the liquid is the consistency of thin maple syrup, about 20 minutes. (Take care not to overcook it, as the syrup will continue to thicken as it cools.) Remove from the heat and let cool. Store in the refrigerator for up to 1 month.

YIELD: ABOUT 1 CUP (235 ML)

Pomegranate Syrup and Pomegranate Molasses

GRENADINE IS A TANGY, SWEET SYRUP MADE FROM POMEGRANATES, although you'd hardly know it from the artificial stuff that passes for grenadine in most grocery stores. Homemade pomegranate syrup is far superior, and can be used in exactly the same way as its mass-produced counterpart. Rich in color and flavor, it can enliven a cocktail, a mocktail, or even a simple glass of seltzer. Pomegranate molasses is a luscious, concentrated form of the syrup, and it's often used as a condiment in Middle Eastern cooking. Its deeper flavor can also complement brown liquors, and it appears in the Pomegranate Molasses Switchel on page 107. (If you plan to make molasses, you might consider doubling the recipe so that you end up with a larger quantity.)

2 cups (470 ml) pomegranate juice (from about 4 pomegranates)
1 tablespoon (15 ml) freshly squeezed lemon juice (from about ½ lemon)
½ cup (100 g) sugar

Combine the pomegranate juice, lemon juice, and sugar in a medium saucepan. (If you use a smaller saucepan, the mixture will take longer to reduce and thicken.) Bring to a simmer over medium-low heat.

To make syrup, simmer for 15 minutes, stirring frequently. Remove from the heat and let cool, or continue cooking to make molasses.

To make molasses, continue cooking the syrup at a gentle, steady simmer, stirring occasionally. Cook until the liquid has reduced to about ³/₄ cup (180 ml) and has the consistency of a thick syrup, about 30 more minutes. (If you feel confident, you can tell whether the syrup's ready simply by eyeballing it, or keep a heat-proof measuring cup handy to help you check your progress from time to time.) The molasses will bubble vigorously near the end. Keep stirring, watch it closely, and take care not to overcook it, because the molasses will continue to thicken as it cools. Remove from the heat and let cool.

Store in the refrigerator for up to 1 month for syrup and 3 months for molasses.

YIELD: ABOUT 2 CUPS SYRUP (470 ML) OR ³/₄ CUP MOLASSES (255 G)

continued on next page

HOW TO EXTRACT POMEGRANATE JUICE

Don't worry: it's surprisingly easy! First, cut the pomegranate in half through the equator. Hold the pomegranate half over a large bowl, cut-side down, and squeeze it to help loosen the seeds. Using a wooden spatula or spoon, whack the back and sides of the pomegranate half. The seeds will fall into the bowl. Continue tapping until you've extracted all the seeds. Discard any bits of membrane that have fallen into the bowl.

To juice the seeds, press them through a food mill or sieve. Or pulse the seeds in a blender or food processor, then strain the juice through a fine-mesh strainer, and discard the solids. (One pomegranate typically yields $1/2$ to $3/4$ cup [120 to 180 ml] juice.)

Variation: You can make syrup and molasses from other fruits, too, like cherries, grapes, and mulberries. Extract the juice (see page 25), then simply use it to replace the pomegranate juice, and continue to follow the Pomegranate Syrup and Pomegranate Molasses recipe on page 83.

OXYMELS, SHRUBS, AND SWITCHELS

DRINKING VINEGARS, SUCH AS OXYMELS, SHRUBS, AND SWITCHELS, have become so popular of late that it might seem as if they were a phenomenon of the modern cocktail bar. But the truth is, people have been imbibing vinegar for thousands of years. To get why that may have happened in the first place, it might help to understand how vinegar is made. Vinegar, at its core, is soured alcohol. Although the word comes from the French *vin aigre*, or "sour wine," vinegar can be made from any type of alcohol, including wine, beer, and cider. When the alcohol is exposed to oxygen it ferments, and *Acetobacter* bacteria transform it into acetic acid: that's what gives vinegar its sour taste.

It's easy to imagine that early drinking and cooking vinegars were simply accidents of wine gone bad. Instead of discarding this tart liquid, though, people came to appreciate its unique qualities. Because of its ability to inhibit the growth of dangerous microbes, vinegar could be used as an antiseptic to make water safe to drink, as well as to preserve precious herbs, fruits, and vegetables. The acetic acid in vinegar can help the body absorb essential minerals—such as calcium—from the foods we eat, and its sour flavor can stimulate saliva production and slake thirst. Vinegar can also extract aromatic compounds and medicinal constituents, such as minerals, from plants.

Folks have been drinking vinegar to reap its health benefits for thousands of years. Around 4000 BCE, the Babylonians fortified their water with vinegar made from date and raisin wines. In ancient China, vinegar made from rice wine was used to promote digestion. Later, the Romans infused vinegar with herbs and mixed it with water to make a beverage called *posca*, which was served to thirsty soldiers. The relationship between vinegar and warriors also existed in feudal Japan, where samurai drank vinegar in preparation for battle.

Of course, not everyone likes vinegar neat. Our ancestors also mixed vinegar with honey, sugar, molasses, and other sweeteners to make healthful syrups and drinks more palatable. In addition to providing sweetness, honey can soothe a sore throat, and its antibacterial properties can promote healing and preserve botanical ingredients. The oxymel, which literally means "acid honey," has been around since antiquity, when Hippocrates prescribed vinegar and honey syrup as an expectorant to ease wet, congested coughs and other ailments. Herbalists have kept the tradition alive throughout the ages, using vinegar and honey to extract, preserve, and administer the beneficial properties of herbs like bee balm, elderberries, garlic, rosemary, sage, and thyme. Depending on how potent an oxymel is, you could sip it neat, dilute it in a cup of hot water, or use it in a cocktail. (One tablespoon [15 ml] is a typical dose for medicinal purposes.)

Another vinegar-based drink is the shrub, which also takes its name from an Arabic syrup, or *sharbât*. (For more on syrups and their history, check out chapter 3.) In contrast to most syrups, however, shrubs are distinctly sour and tangy. They almost always contain fruit, and, at one time, were an effective way to preserve the bounty of the summer harvest. Nineteenth- and early twentieth-century American housekeeping manuals are filled with recipes for raspberry, cherry, and other varieties of shrubs—drinks that became particularly popular during the Temperance movement, because they were nonalcoholic yet zippy and refreshing. Although several methods exist for making shrubs, the most common process involves creating a fruit-flavored vinegar and sweetening it with sugar. The easiest way to serve a shrub is to simply mix it with sparkling water to make a tangy, grown-up soda.

Then there's our friend the switchel. This vinegar-based drink has its roots in the Caribbean islands, where it was most likely made with vinegar, ginger, molasses, water, and perhaps rum in the sixteenth and seventeenth centuries. As the molasses trade traveled to New England, so did switchels. There they became known as haymaker's punch for their ability to quench workers' thirst as they labored during the harvest—just like a modern-day sports drink.

Vinegar drinks such as oxymels, shrubs, and switchels are a fun way to get creative with all kinds of fruits and herbs, from blackberries to spruce tips and shiso leaves. Even better, they're easy to make. I had fun envisioning some new versions of these classic drinks, and I think you'll enjoy them, too!

Crafting Vinegar Drinks

ALWAYS INFUSE VINEGARS IN VERY clean containers—at the very least, make sure they've been thoroughly washed with hot, soapy water. You can also sanitize (see page 19) or sterilize (see page 18) them to be extra-safe, which is an especially good idea if you're using fresh fruit or herbs. Fresh ingredients should always be completely submerged in the vinegar to prevent spoilage: if they have a tendency to float, shaking the jar daily will ensure that they soak evenly.

Vinegar drinks can be made with just about any vinegar—with two caveats. Number one: avoid distilled white vinegar. It's great for household cleaning, but not homemade beverages. Number two: if you plan to leave the vinegar outside the refrigerator to infuse, always use vinegar with a 5 percent or higher acidity to ensure safe preservation. Acidity information can usually be found on the bottle's label. If you're using homemade vinegar, you'll need to test the acidity, or just keep the infusion in the refrigerator. Use these vinegars to make oxymels, shrubs, and switchels:

- **Apple cider vinegar** is a great go-to vinegar for any preparations that involve fruit, and its round flavor is an especially good match for fruits like apples, pears, peaches, and plums. Raw, unfiltered apple cider vinegar retains the nutritional benefits that can be lost in processing, making it the vinegar of choice for many herbal and health-oriented drinks.

- **White wine vinegar and Champagne vinegar** have crisp, clean flavors that also work well with fruits and berries.

- **Red wine vinegar** imparts a lovely color that can complement berries, such as red currants and raspberries. For a smoother taste, try mixing it with Champagne vinegar.

- **Balsamic vinegar** is thick and rich, and goes especially well with berries like cherries and strawberries.

- **Rice vinegar** is light and delicate and is often delicious with herbs. Note, however, that it has less than 5 percent acidity.

- **Coconut vinegar** may complement tropical fruits, ginger, and turmeric, although I find its taste a bit harsh.

Most drinking vinegars can last for a year or even longer in the refrigerator, especially if you sterilize the container as directed on page 18. That said, use your own judgment. If the vinegar is bubbling or if it looks moldy, cloudy, or slimy, throw it out.

Kitchen Tip: Vinegar can corrode metal. When using a metal lid with an infusing jar, place a piece of plastic wrap, waxed paper, or parchment paper between the jar and the lid to prevent it from corroding.

Blackberry and Thyme Oxymel

ALTHOUGH OXYMELS ARE TYPICALLY MADE WITH HERBS, THEY CAN ALSO incorporate fruits, especially berries like blackberries or raspberries. Here, blackberries boost the oxymel's flavor and provide vitamin C and valuable antioxidants. Fragrant thyme not only complements the blackberries but can also relieve coughs and clear up chest congestion. Enjoy this sweet and tangy syrup in a cup of tea, or use it to make a homemade soda. It's also an easy way to add the complexity of sweet berry and herbal notes to a salad dressing.

1¼ cups (180 g) blackberries
½ cup (20 g) fresh thyme leaves or ¼ cup (11 g) dried
1 cup (235 ml) apple cider vinegar
¾ cup (255 g) honey

Place the blackberries in a bowl and lightly crush them using a potato masher or fork.

Combine the blackberries, their juices, and the thyme in a sterilized pint (470 ml) jar. Pour the vinegar into the jar. Leave at least ¹/₄ inch (6 mm) of headspace and make sure the berries and herbs are completely submerged.

Wipe the rim of the jar with a clean cloth. Cover the jar with a nonreactive lid (see page 89). Store the jar in a cool, dark place for 2 to 4 weeks, shaking it daily and ensuring that the berries and herbs stay submerged. Strain the mixture through a fine-mesh strainer lined with a flour sack (beware: the berry mixture will stain!). Discard the solids. Combine the strained vinegar and honey in a sterilized jar or bottle, cover it with a nonreactive lid, and shake to combine. Store in the refrigerator for up to 1 year.

YIELD: ABOUT 1¹/₂ CUPS (355 ML)

Wildcrafting Tip: Look for blackberry (*Rubus* spp.) patches near rivers, streams, and even urban areas with sufficient water. To protect yourself from thorns, wear long pants and sleeves. Berries are ripe when they are soft and come easily off the vine. Simply taste a few of them in different stages of color and firmness and you'll soon learn what to look for.

Sage Oxymel

THIS AROMATIC OXYMEL IS THE VERY FIRST ONE I EVER MADE AND, years later, it's still one of my favorites. Sage's botanical name, *Salvia*, comes from the Latin word meaning "to heal" or "to save," and many cultures have long valued the plant's ability to relieve cold and flu symptoms, aid the digestion of rich foods, and enhance memory. There's nothing quite like it for soothing an inflamed sore throat or easing a congested cough—and it's also great for jogging the brain and perking up the senses. Take it by the teaspoonful, or turn it into a restorative tea by adding a splash to a cup of hot water.

2 cups (80 g) fresh sage leaves, chopped, or 1 cup (32 g) dried
¾ cup (255 g) honey
1 cup (235 ml) apple cider vinegar

Combine the sage and honey in a sterilized pint (470 ml) jar. Gradually pour in the vinegar, stirring with a chopstick to release air bubbles and moisten the sage. Leave at least ¼ inch (6 mm) of headspace and make sure any fresh sage is completely submerged.

Wipe the rim of the jar with a clean cloth. Cover the jar with a nonreactive lid (see page 89). Store the jar in a cool, dark place for 2 to 4 weeks, shaking it daily and ensuring that the sage stays submerged. Strain the mixture through a fine-mesh strainer. Discard the solids. Transfer to a sterilized container with a nonreactive lid. Store in the refrigerator for up to 1 year.

YIELD: ABOUT 1½ CUPS (355 ML)

 Botanical Note: Feel free to use common garden sage (*Salvia officinalis*) or an aromatic wild sage. I'm especially fond of my local, native black sage (*Salvia mellifera*) and purple sage (*Salvia leucophylla*). However, wild sage can be more pungent than its domesticated cousin, so if you're using it, avoid a bitter oxymel by using less sage (I use about half as much), and by decreasing the mixture's infusion time.

Fire Cider

HORSERADISH, GARLIC, GINGER, ONIONS, AND CHILE PEPPERS FORM THE basis of this vinegar tonic, and I admit it: the combination sounds pretty frightening! In fact, it took me years to work up the courage to try it—but now, a shot of Fire Cider is one of the first things I reach for to ward off a cold or flu, relieve sinus congestion, and warm up on a cold day. Hot, pungent, sour, and sweet, Fire Cider was formulated by herbalist Rosemary Gladstar as a robust immune enhancer that anyone can make in his or her own kitchen. Gladstar has encouraged people to adapt Fire Cider to their own tastes, and by sharing this recipe, I hope you will do the same. I usually add turmeric and citrus to Gladstar's core recipe, plus wild chiles pequíns that my mother forages in her Texas backyard. Depending on my mood and on what's in season, I sometimes throw in a chopped beet, a handful of parsley, or some rose hips.

½ cup (75 g) peeled, finely chopped garlic (about 10 cloves)

½ cup (about 4 ounces, or 112 g) peeled, finely chopped horseradish

½ cup (80 g) peeled, finely chopped onion (about 1 medium)

¼ cup (about 2 ounces, or 56 g) peeled, finely chopped fresh ginger

¼ cup (about 2 ounces, or 56 g) peeled, finely chopped fresh turmeric or 1 heaping tablespoon (7 g) ground turmeric

1 small orange (preferably a blood orange), quartered and thinly sliced crosswise

½ lemon, quartered and thinly sliced crosswise

1 habanero chile, or 2 chiles pequíns, or ⅛ teaspoon ground cayenne

½ teaspoon black peppercorns

2 to 3 cups (470 to 705 ml) apple cider vinegar

2 tablespoons to ½ cup (40 to 170 g) honey, to taste

Combine the garlic, horseradish, onion, ginger, turmeric, orange, lemon, chile, and peppercorns in a sterilized quart (1 L) jar. Pour the vinegar into the jar, stirring with a chopstick to release air bubbles. Leave ½ inch (1.3 cm) of headspace and make sure the ingredients are submerged.

Wipe the rim of the jar with a clean cloth. Cover the jar with a nonreactive lid (see page 89). Store the jar in a cool, dark place for 1 month, shaking it daily and ensuring that the ingredients stay submerged. Strain through a fine-mesh strainer into a bowl, pressing on the solids to extract as much liquid as possible. Discard the solids. Whisk in the honey to taste; I usually like about 2 tablespoons (40 g), but some folks like as much as ¹/₂ cup (170 g). Transfer to a sterilized bottle with a nonreactive lid. Store in the refrigerator for up to 1 year.

YIELD: ABOUT 2 CUPS (470 ML)

Fire Cider Hot Toddy

ALTHOUGH IT'S PRIMARILY A HEALTH TONIC, FIRE CIDER CAN ADD plenty of kick to your cocktails, too. The savory, vinegar-based concoction is a natural addition to a Bloody Mary and pairs well with the spice in a rye whiskey, or the smokiness in mezcal or tequila reposado. You can use Fire Cider by the dash, like bitters, or, for serious spice lovers, by the shot. When you're making this Fire Cider Hot Toddy, you may want to play around with the proportions a bit, depending upon how sweet your Fire Cider is. One thing's for sure, though: it's as good as an extra blanket on a cold night!

¼ ounce (7 g) honey (or more, to taste)

¾ ounce (23 ml) Fire Cider (page 92)

1½ ounces (45 ml) rye whiskey, mezcal, or tequila reposado

½ cup (120 ml) hot water

Lemon slice

Combine the honey, Fire Cider, and liquor in a mug. Top with hot water and stir. Garnish with a lemon slice.

YIELD: 1 SERVING

Evergreen Oxymel

MIXOLOGISTS AND HERBALISTS LOVE EVERGREEN CONIFERS NOT ONLY for their piney, sometimes citrusy flavors, but also for their antioxidants; their ability to warm up a chilly body; and the way they can break up a boggy, chesty cough. You can make this oxymel with any edible conifer, such as pine (*Pinus* spp.), spruce (*Picea* spp.), fir (*Abies* spp.), or Douglas fir (*Pseudotsuga menziesii*). After steeping the needles in vinegar, you'll wind up with a flavored vinegar that's delicious all by itself (pine needle vinegar is often compared to balsamic vinegar). You might wish to reserve some for cooking; as for the rest, you'll mix it with honey to make a tasty, healing oxymel.

2 large handfuls conifer needles
1 cup (235 ml) apple cider vinegar
¾ cup (255 g) honey, or to taste

Roughly cut the conifer needles using scissors or a heavy knife. Combine the needles and vinegar in a sterilized pint (470 ml) jar, stirring with a chopstick to release air bubbles and moisten all the needles. Leave at least $^1/_4$ inch (6 mm) of headspace and make sure the needles are completely submerged.

Wipe the rim of the jar with a clean cloth. Cover the jar with a nonreactive lid (see page 89). Store the jar in a cool, dark place for 2 to 4 weeks, shaking it daily and ensuring that the needles stay submerged. Strain the mixture through a fine-mesh strainer lined with a cloth or towel; discard the solids. Combine the strained vinegar and honey in a sterilized jar or bottle, cover it with a nonreactive lid, and shake to combine. Store in the refrigerator for up to 1 year.

YIELD: ABOUT 1$^1/_2$ CUPS (355 ML)

Wildcrafting Tip: Conifer needles or leaves may be harvested any time of year, although they're usually most aromatic in spring and can be bitter in winter, so pick accordingly. And, I know I've said it before, but I can't overemphasize how important it is to taste each individual tree, because their flavors really do vary! Also, be sure not to harvest too much from any single tree; move around and gather a little here and there to maintain the area's ecological balance.

Mint Sekanjabin

FIRST MENTIONED IN THE TENTH-CENTURY *FIHRIST OF AL-NADIM*, a catalog of books in Arabic, *sekanjabin* is the medieval Persian version of oxymel. It probably originated as a simple preparation of honey and vinegar, since the word *sekanjabin* derives from the words *serke* ("vinegar") and *angobin* ("honey"). Today, sekanjabin is typically perfumed with mint and used as a dipping sauce for crisp lettuce leaves–a healthy, refreshing snack that can take the edge off a hot day. I like to make sekanjabin with a mild honey, such as orange blossom, but sugar works well here, too. Apple cider vinegar, lemon juice, or lime juice could stand in for the white wine vinegar, and the mint could be replaced with another mint-family herb, such as lemon balm (*Melissa officinalis*) or bee balm (*Monarda didyma*).

1⅓ cups mild honey (452 g) or 2 cups sugar (400 g)

1 cup (235 ml) water

½ cup (120 ml) white wine vinegar

1 cup (96 g) loosely packed fresh
   mint leaves

Combine the honey and water in a saucepan. Bring to a boil over medium-low heat, stirring to dissolve the honey. Reduce the heat to low and simmer gently for 5 minutes. Add the vinegar and continue simmering for 20 minutes, or until the mixture thickens to a syrupy consistency. Remove from the heat and skim off any foam. Stir in the mint. Let cool completely. Strain the mixture through a fine-mesh strainer; discard the solids. Transfer to a sterilized container with a nonreactive lid (see page 89). Store in the refrigerator for up to 1 month.

YIELD: ABOUT 1 ³/₄ CUPS (411 ML)

Cucumber and Mint Cooler

WITH COOL, JUICY CUCUMBER MAKES IT EVEN MORE REFRESHING.
If you can, use small Persian cucumbers, which are crisp, slightly sweet, and devoid of tough seeds. These cucumbers have delicate skins, so peeling is optional. Can't find them? Long, slender English cucumbers make a good substitute.

1¼ ounces (37.5 ml) Mint Sekanjabin (page 96)

¼ ounce (7.5 ml) fresh lime juice

2 tablespoons (15 g) grated cucumber (preferably Persian cucumber)

Ice cubes

1½ ounces (45 ml) white rum (optional)

6 ounces (180 ml) club soda, chilled

Fresh mint sprig, for garnish

In a tall glass, stir together the Mint Sekanjabin, lime juice, and grated cucumber. Fill the glass with ice and stir in the rum and club soda. Garnish with the mint, and serve immediately.

YIELD: 1 SERVING

Cherry Balsamic Shrub

OUT OF ALL OF THE SHRUBS I MAKE, THIS MARRIAGE OF CHERRIES, BALSAMIC vinegar, and vanilla bean is always the most popular. I love the bit of luxury it brings to everything it touches! Because balsamic vinegar can be overwhelming on its own (not to mention pricey), I mix it with white vinegar here—and I use raw turbinado sugar, too, which adds a richness that's missing from ordinary sugar. Stirred into sparkling water, the Cherry Balsamic Shrub becomes a grown-up cherry cream soda. As for cocktails, it mixes particularly well with bourbon. And don't forget the possibilities when it comes to ice cream: toss a teaspoon or so over a bowl of good-quality vanilla, and dessert is served.

2 cups (310 g) pitted sweet cherries
1 cup (235 ml) balsamic vinegar
1 cup (235 ml) white wine vinegar
1 vanilla bean, split
2 cups (384 g) turbinado sugar

Place the cherries in a bowl and lightly crush them using a potato masher or a fork. Transfer the cherries and their juices to a sterilized quart (1 L) jar. Pour the balsamic vinegar and white wine vinegar into the jar, making sure the cherries are completely submerged. Tuck the vanilla bean into the vinegar, too.

Wipe the rim of the jar with a clean cloth. Cover the jar with a nonreactive lid (see page 89). Store the jar in a cool, dark place for 1 week, shaking it daily and ensuring that the cherries and vanilla stay submerged. Strain the mixture through a fine-mesh strainer. Discard the solids. Combine the vinegar and sugar in a sterilized container with a nonreactive lid. Refrigerate for 1 week more, shaking the jar daily to help dissolve the sugar. Store in the refrigerator for up to 1 year.

YIELD: ABOUT 2 CUPS (470 ML)

Kitchen Tip: Grinding turbinado sugar into smaller crystals will help it dissolve more quickly. To do so, use a clean food processor, coffee grinder, or mortar and pestle.

Raspberry Shrub

RASPBERRY SHRUBS OFTEN POP UP IN NINETEENTH- AND EARLY TWENTIETH-century American housekeeping manuals, and those early recipes inspired the version you see here. And the result is a winner: it's beautifully vibrant in both color and flavor. Of course, there's still plenty of room for experimentation, so you could easily substitute another berry, or try out a different kind of vinegar: a mix of red wine vinegar and Champagne vinegar is my preferred choice for raspberries, but all-red or all-Champagne works, too.

2 cups (250 g) raspberries
1 cup (235 ml) Champagne vinegar
1 cup (235 ml) red wine vinegar
2 cups (400 g) sugar

Place the raspberries in a bowl and lightly crush them using a potato masher or a fork. Transfer the raspberries and their juices to a sterilized quart (1 L) jar. Pour the Champagne vinegar and red wine vinegar into the jar, making sure the raspberries are completely submerged.

Wipe the rim of the jar with a clean cloth. Cover the jar with a nonreactive lid (see page 89). Store the jar in a cool, dark place for 1 week, shaking it daily and ensuring that the raspberries stay submerged. Strain the mixture through a fine-mesh strainer; discard the solids. Combine the vinegar and sugar in a sterilized container with a nonreactive lid. Refrigerate for 1 week more, shaking the jar daily to help dissolve the sugar. Store in the refrigerator for up to 1 year.

YIELD: ABOUT 2 CUPS (470 ML)

Serving Suggestion: To make a simple cocktail with any shrub, including this Raspberry Shrub, combine 2 ounces (60 ml) liquor with ³/₄ ounce (23 ml) shrub syrup in a Collins or highball glass, and top with club soda. Adjust to taste. It's that easy!

WILD DRINKS AND COCKTAILS

Classic Switchel

ORIGINATING IN THE CARIBBEAN BEFORE MAKING ITS WAY TO NEW England, the switchel has developed into different versions over the years. My exploration has turned up an array of different ingredients and ratios—but, in general, a switchel was likely to contain the sweet, tangy, and spicy combination of molasses, vinegar, and ginger. Together, these components provide valuable minerals and electrolytes, which means that the humble switchel is a great alternative to commercially made sports drinks. Or, if you want to skip the work-out and head straight to the bar, you'll find that rum is a great partner for this bracing concoction.

2 tablespoons (40 g) molasses (preferably blackstrap)

1 tablespoon (15 ml) apple cider vinegar

1 teaspoon grated fresh ginger

1 cup (235 ml) water

Combine the molasses, apple cider vinegar, and ginger in a jar or glass and stir to dilute the molasses. Add the water and stir to combine.

Cover and refrigerate for at least 2 hours and up to a day. The longer it steeps, the stronger the ginger flavor will be. Strain through a fine-mesh strainer; discard the solids. Serve over ice.

YIELD: 1 CUP (235 ML)

Switchel Cocktail

THIS ROBUST COCKTAIL INCORPORATES RUM AS A COMPLEMENT TO THE molasses in the switchel—after all, most rum is made from molasses—and it's a nod to the Caribbean origins of both. Coat the rim of the cocktail glass with turbinado sugar crystals: it's a fun counterpoint to the dark brown color of the molasses and rum, and to the vinegar's tanginess. (If you prefer a simpler drink, though, go ahead and skip the sugar-coated rim.) What I love most about the Switchel Cocktail is that it's a year-round hit. During the winter, the flavors of molasses and aromatic bitters make it just the thing for holiday gatherings; sipped in summer, it evokes warm, sunny days in the Caribbean islands.

Lime wedge

Turbinado sugar

2 ounces (60 ml) Classic Switchel (page 102)

2 ounces (60 ml) dark rum

½ ounce (15 ml) fresh lime juice

2 dashes aromatic bitters

Ice

Moisten the rim of a cocktail glass with a lime wedge and coat with turbinado sugar. Combine the Classic Switchel, rum, lime juice, and bitters in a cocktail shaker. Add ice and shake well. Fill the prepared glass with ice and strain in the cocktail. Serve immediately.

YIELD: 1 SERVING

Shiso Vinegar

AS A CHILD, I USED TO SIT IN MY FATHER'S VIETNAMESE HERB GARDEN, marveling at the *tiá tô* leaves that were green on top and purple underneath. When you rubbed them between your fingers, they released a heady aroma of mint, coriander, and cinnamon. Also known as shiso (*Perilla frutescens*), species of this mint-family herb may be found in Chinese, Japanese, and Korean markets, and in fields in the eastern United States and Canada, where they have become invasive garden escapees. Some varieties are purely green, but for this recipe, you'll want to use a type that's partially or completely purple or red, such as the Vietnamese *tía tô* or milder-tasting Japanese *akajiso*. Boil the leaves, add vinegar to the water, and behold: the mixture will turn the most glorious shade of pink you've ever seen!

1 cup (235 ml) water

1 cup (4 ounces, or 112 g) red shiso leaves

1 cup (235 ml) rice vinegar

1 cup (200 g) sugar

Bring the water to a boil in a small saucepan. Stir in the shiso leaves. Reduce the heat and simmer, uncovered, for 5 minutes. Remove from the heat and let stand for 5 minutes. Strain through a fine-mesh strainer and squeeze the leaves to extract all the liquid; discard the leaves.

Return the liquid to the saucepan and add the vinegar and sugar; the liquid will turn pink. Bring to a simmer over medium-low heat, stirring to dissolve the sugar. Simmer for another minute. Remove from the heat and let cool. Transfer to a sterilized container with a nonreactive lid (see page 89). Store in the refrigerator for up to 1 month.

YIELD: 2 CUPS (470 ML)

Serving Suggestion: Make a restorative soda by mixing 1 part shiso vinegar with 4 parts sparkling water. Adjust to taste, and serve immediately.

Haymaker's Punch

WHEN IT REACHED NEW ENGLAND, THE SWITCHEL BECAME KNOWN AS "haymaker's punch," thanks to its ability to quench laborers' thirst during the heavy work of harvesting. Instead of molasses, New Englanders often sweetened the drink with an ingredient more readily available to them: maple syrup. In addition to its inimitable flavor, maple syrup supplies parched bodies with minerals such as manganese, zinc, potassium, and iron. Inspired by early recipes, this switchel also incorporates oatmeal for extra texture and nutrition. That might make Haymaker's Punch sound more like a breakfast food than a drink, but don't be put off: it's surprisingly refreshing and energizing.

1 tablespoon (15 ml) pure maple syrup, or more to taste

1 tablespoon (15 ml) apple cider vinegar

1 teaspoon freshly squeezed lemon juice

1 teaspoon grated fresh ginger

1 tablespoon (5 g) rolled oats

1 cup (235 ml) water

Ice

Combine the maple syrup, apple cider vinegar, lemon juice, and ginger in a jar or glass and stir to dilute the maple syrup. Add the oats and water and stir to combine. Cover and refrigerate for at least 2 hours and up to a day. The longer it steeps, the stronger the ginger flavor will be.

Strain the mixture through a fine-mesh strainer; discard the solids. Taste and sweeten with additional maple syrup, if desired. Serve over ice.

YIELD: 1 OR 2 SERVINGS

Pomegranate Molasses Switchel

HERE'S AN EXAMPLE OF HOW YOU CAN SWITCH UP THE BASIC SWITCHEL formula. Just swap the apple cider vinegar for balsamic vinegar, and the molasses for pomegranate molasses: give the mixture a shake, and you've got a tangy, sweet drink that makes a great mid-afternoon thirst quencher or mocktail. If you're not planning on making your own pomegranate molasses, never fear: you can often find it at Middle Eastern markets and well-stocked supermarkets. Also, when it comes to the balsamic vinegar, now is not the time to use the cheap stuff. Be sure to use the best-quality balsamic you can afford; it's true that the recipe only calls for a small amount, but trust me, you'll notice the difference.

1 tablespoon (20 g) pomegranate molasses, homemade (page 83) or store-bought

2 teaspoons sugar or honey, or more to taste

1 teaspoon balsamic vinegar

1 teaspoon grated fresh ginger

1 cup (235 ml) water

Ice

Combine all the ingredients in a jar, cover, and shake to dissolve the pomegranate molasses. Refrigerate for at least 2 hours and up to a day. The longer it steeps, the stronger the ginger flavor will be. Taste and sweeten with additional sugar or honey, if desired.

Shake until foamy. Strain through a fine-mesh strainer into 1 or 2 ice-filled glasses; discard the solids. Serve immediately.

YIELD: 1 OR 2 SERVINGS

Turmeric Switchel

THIS BRIGHT NEW RIFF ON THE CLASSIC SWITCHEL FEATURES TURMERIC, which is a powerful anti-inflammatory and antiviral agent. I highly recommend using fresh turmeric, which has a livelier flavor than the dried version. Look for the fresh rhizomes, which resemble orange knobs of ginger root, at health food stores or at well-stocked grocery stores and Asian and Indian markets. For an extra-spicy kick, add a tiny pinch of black pepper to the Turmeric Switchel: it'll increase the bioavailability of curcumin, an anti-inflammatory compound found in turmeric.

1 tablespoon (20 g) honey, or more to taste

1 tablespoon (15 ml) apple cider vinegar

½ teaspoon freshly squeezed lime juice

1 teaspoon grated fresh turmeric or ⅓ teaspoon dried

1 teaspoon grated fresh ginger

Tiny pinch of freshly ground black pepper (optional)

1 cup (235 ml) water

Ice

Combine the honey, apple cider vinegar, lime juice, turmeric, ginger, and black pepper in a jar or glass and stir to dilute the honey. Add the water and stir to combine. Cover and refrigerate for at least 2 hours and up to a day. The longer it steeps, the stronger the turmeric and ginger flavors will be.

Strain the mixture through a fine-mesh strainer; discard the solids. Taste and sweeten with additional honey, if desired. Serve over ice.

YIELD: 1 OR 2 SERVINGS

> **Kitchen Tip:** Fresh turmeric can stain clothes and other items, so be careful if you're grating it on or around porous kitchen surfaces and tools. Wear an apron, too!

Turmeric Switchel Cocktail

TURMERIC SWITCHEL'S PIQUANT TANG BLENDS SO WELL WITH FRESH-
tasting sugarcane spirits, like a good-quality cachaça. One caveat, though: when you're preparing a Turmeric Switchel for use in mixed drinks, you'll want to sweeten it with more honey (I usually increase the amount of honey to 1½ tablespoons, or 30 g).

3 ounces (90 ml) Turmeric Switchel (page 108)

Simple Syrup (page 51) or Honey Syrup (page 52), optional

1½ ounces (45 ml) cachaça

Ice

Lime wheel, for garnish

Combine the Turmeric Switchel, syrup, and cachaça in a cocktail shaker. Add ice and shake well. Strain into an ice-filled highball glass. Garnish with a lime wheel.

YIELD: 1 SERVING

> **Variation:** Want to add a little greenery to your cocktail? Muddle a lime wedge and a small handful of cilantro leaves, chickweed (*Stellaria media*), or young dandelion (*Taraxacum officinale*) leaves in the bottom of the cocktail shaker before adding the other ingredients. Then garnish the finished drink with fresh herbs.

INFUSIONS, BITTERS, AND LIQUEURS

W HEN IT COMES TO MAKING INFUSED LIQUORS, THE FLAVOR possibilities are truly endless. Got wild elderberries or figs? You're already on your way to a sweet liqueur. Chamomile flowers? Let's make bitters! Juniper berries? Time for gin.

Many infused liquors or spirits originated as medicinal preparations. Simple infusions involve steeping herbs, spices, or fruits in alcohol, which not only preserves the plant material but also extracts the flavor and herbal constituents. Infusions can be sipped neat, but they're more often used as mixers in cocktails. When made with single ingredients for medicinal or culinary purposes, these infusions are sometimes called tinctures, while sweetened infusions are known as liqueurs. Liqueurs can be used in cocktails or enjoyed on their own, often as a digestif. As for elixirs, it's a term herbalists use for a liqueur that's (usually) made with brandy and sweetened with honey—a heck of a nice way to take your medicine!

Infusions made with bitter-tasting herbs are called—yes, you guessed it—bitters. Bitter herbs that turn up in bitters include roots, barks, and leaves like angelica root, artichoke leaf, burdock root, citrus peel, dandelion root and leaf, gentian root, horehound, mugwort, wormwood, and yellow dock root. A lot of wild edible plants taste bitter, making them ideal ingredients for home-crafted bitters. To round out the flavor of the bitters, you can add other herbs, spices, fruits, berries, flowers, or nuts of your choice to the mix, as well as minimal amounts of syrups or sweeteners.

Health practitioners have long used bitter foods and drinks to support digestion, because the bitter taste stimulates the body's natural ability to digest carbohydrates,

fats, and more. It also helps regulate blood sugar. In England and colonial America, bitters and medicinal tonics formulated by physicians often included carminative (gas-relieving) herbs, too. These digestive bitters made their way to the bar, where they became essential to the cocktail, since just a few drops or dashes of bitters can add balance and depth of flavor and aroma to a drink. In fact, in 1806, according to the New York newspaper *The Balance and Columbian Repository*, the very definition of a cocktail was "a stimulating liquor, composed of spirits of any kind, sugar, water and bitters."

Bitter herbs aren't confined to making bitters, though: they're also used to make bittersweet liqueurs. These boast a long history in Europe, particularly Italy and France, where the tradition is still strong. There, aperitif and digestif liqueurs are made with ingredients such as bitter roots, citrus, artichoke, rhubarb, and various other local botanicals. Like bitter infusions, these liqueurs can be added to soda and cocktails, but they can also be sipped neat.

Juniper-flavored gin is another liquor with a venerable medicinal history, having been formulated by a Dutch physician in the seventeenth century. Gin can be made a few different ways. Distilled gin is the type you usually buy at the liquor store, but you can also make your own compound gin by infusing a neutral spirit, such as vodka, with juniper berries and other botanicals.

Crafting Infused Liquors

ALWAYS INFUSE LIQUORS IN CLEAN CONTAINERS THAT ARE, AT THE VERY least, thoroughly washed with hot, soapy water. You can also sanitize (see page 19) or sterilize (see page 18) your containers for extra insurance, which is an especially good idea if you're using fresh fruit or herbs. Fresh ingredients should always be completely submerged under the alcohol to prevent spoilage. When they have a tendency to float, shaking the jar daily can ensure that the fruit or herbs stay evenly soaked in alcohol.

Some people advise using the cheapest base spirit you can find when you're making your own infused liquors, but I recommend using a mid-range-quality alcohol. There's no need to splurge on a top-shelf brand, but the spirit itself should still be palatable.

Here's a quick rundown of the types of spirits you'll be using:

- **Vodka** is distilled from grains, potatoes, or beets, and its neutral flavor makes it a good base for infusions of all kinds.

- **Brandy** is distilled from fruit wine. It's typically made from grapes, but can also be made from apples, pears, and other fruits. Brandy can really complement fruit infusions. In this case, it's a good idea to spend a little more on your base spirit. Use an aged brandy (labeled XO or VSOP) for a smoother sip.

- **Gin's** distinctive juniper flavor can be tricky when it comes to making infusions, so use it with care—but it does complement some herbs and fruits, such as blackberries, blueberries, plums, cucumbers, ginger, rosemary, and sage.

- **Rum** is distilled from sugarcane or molasses. Light or white rum is generally a good choice for ingredients such as citrus or berries, and darker rums work well with stone fruits, nuts, and spices.

- **Tequila** is distilled from the agave cactus. Unaged (blanco) tequila is generally a nice pairing for ingredients like tropical fruits or chiles, although aged tequilas can also be interesting with chiles and citrus fruits.

- **Whiskey** is distilled from grain, and its character depends on whether it's made with barley, rye, or corn, and on how long it's been aged. Bourbon has a sweet vanilla flavor that can work with many fruit infusions, like cherries, figs, and apples, while Scotch and rye are good choices for bitters, thanks to their smoky or spicy flavors.

How can you determine the strength of a spirit? Well, alcohol content is expressed in two ways: percentage and proof. "Proof" is the spirit's percentage multiplied by two. For example, a vodka that's 40 percent alcohol by volume (ABV) is 80-proof. Most of the recipes in this chapter should be made with 80-proof alcohol, which is strong enough to extract flavors from fruit and herbs and prevent the growth of harmful microorganisms. Higher-proof alcohol, such as Everclear, can extract flavor more quickly and may have a longer shelf life; however, to make it drinkable, you might need to dilute or sweeten it. Adding other liquids to your alcohol, such as simple syrup or fruit juice, will increase the ratio of water in the mixture, thereby reducing the ABV and proof. Most liqueurs are somewhere between 20 and 75 percent ABV, while bitters are around 40 to 45 percent ABV.

Sweetening your infusion can be done in two ways: either by adding sugar or syrup to the mix during the infusion process, or by adding it afterward. Simple Syrup (page 51) is the most neutral—and therefore the most versatile—sweetener, but other sweeteners like honey can lend their own character to the liqueur.

Summer Gin

IT'S ENTIRELY POSSIBLE TO MAKE YOUR OWN GIN: NO DISTILLERY OR bathtub required. As long as the infusion includes juniper berries—which have long been used to stimulate the kidneys, heal urinary tract infections, and treat indigestion, inflammation, colds, and flu—you can call it gin. The hyssop (*Hyssopus officinalis*) provides a bittersweet, floral, minty flavor, while orris root (*Iris germanica*) lends a lovely, violet-like aroma. I call this one Summer Gin because it's so bright and fresh.

2 tablespoons (10 g) dried juniper berries

1 bottle (750 ml, or 3¼ cups) vodka

1 teaspoon dried hyssop

1 teaspoon dried, cut, and sifted orris root

1 teaspoon dried rose petals

½ teaspoon dried lavender flowers

½ teaspoon dried, cut, and sifted lemon peel

½ teaspoon dried elderflowers

4 green cardamom pods

½ dried California bay leaf or 1 dried Turkish bay leaf, torn into pieces

Place the juniper berries in a quart (1 L) jar. Pour the vodka into the jar. Cap the jar tightly. Let stand for 8 hours. Add the rest of the ingredients to the jar, cap, and let stand for 36 hours.

Strain through a fine-mesh strainer lined with a coffee filter or flour sack cloth to remove all fine particles. Discard the solids. Bottle and store in a cool, dark place for up to 1 year.

YIELD: 3¼ CUPS (750 ML)

NOTE:

Homemade compound gin will be darker in color than commercial distilled gin; depending on the botanicals you use, it'll probably be yellow or even golden.

Wildcrafting Tip: Juniper "berries" are actually little cones—like pinecones—and should be harvested when they're ripe, having turned from green to dark blue or purple. Not all species of juniper are suitable for consumption. *Juniperus communis* is the most commonly used species. Avoid savin juniper (*J. sabina*) and prickly juniper (*J. oxycedrus*). Research other species before using them in recipes.

Winter Gin

NOT EVERYONE LOVES THE FACT THAT GIN CAN TASTE LIKE A CHRISTMAS tree, but as someone who treasures the time she spends in conifer forests, I adore it. And this compound gin embraces the Christmas tree spirit full-on. In it, the juniper berries are infused for longer than they are in the Summer Gin on page 114, then they're topped with a fragrant sprig of white fir (*Abies concolor*) and warm, wintery herbs and spices. (If there's no white fir in your area, substitute another local conifer, such as pine or spruce.) Wrap yourself in a flannel blanket, light the fire in your log cabin, and pour yourself a restorative dose.

2 tablespoons (10 g) juniper berries

1 bottle (750 ml, or 3¼ cups) vodka

2 teaspoons coriander seeds

1 teaspoon dried, cut, and sifted orange peel

3-inch (7.5 cm) sprig fresh white fir or ½ sprig dried

1-inch (2.5 cm) cinnamon stick

1 whole allspice berry

1 dried sage leaf

½ dried California bay leaf or 1 dried Turkish bay leaf, torn into pieces

Place the juniper berries in a quart (1 L) jar. Pour the vodka into the jar. Cap the jar tightly. Let it stand for 12 hours. Add the rest of the ingredients to the jar, cap it, and let it stand for 36 hours.

Strain the mixture through a fine-mesh strainer lined with a coffee filter or flour sack cloth to remove all fine particles; discard the solids. Bottle and store in a cool, dark place for up to 1 year.

YIELD: 3¼ CUPS (750 ML)

NOTE:

As with the Summer Gin recipe on page 114, your homemade compound gin will be darker in color than commercial distilled gin; expect it to be yellow or golden.

Chamomile Whisky Bitters

I GOT THE IDEA FOR THESE BITTERS FROM AN OLD RECIPE FOR "HIGHLAND Bitters," published in *A Country Cup* by Wilma Paterson, which were made with Scotch whisky and chamomile. Chamomile (*Matricaria chamomilla, Chamaemelum nobile*) is a gentle yet powerful flower that's renowned for supporting the digestive and nervous systems. You'll find it often used in tea blends to ease stress, insomnia, and indigestion.

2½ tablespoons (4 g) dried chamomile flowers

1 tablespoon (4 g) dried, cut, and sifted orange peel

1½ teaspoons dried, cut, and sifted gentian root

1 teaspoon dried, cut, and sifted lemon peel

2 whole allspice berries

2 whole cloves

3-inch (7.5 cm) cinnamon stick

2 cups (470 ml) Scotch whisky

2 tablespoons (40 g) honey, or to taste

Combine the chamomile, orange peel, gentian, lemon peel, allspice, cloves, cinnamon, and whisky in a quart (1 L) jar. Cap the jar tightly. Store it in a cool, dark place for 2 weeks, shaking daily.

Strain the mixture through a fine-mesh strainer lined with a coffee filter or flour sack cloth. Discard the solids. Combine the strained whisky and honey in a clean jar. Cap the jar tightly and shake it to dissolve the honey. Age for at least 1 week, or for up to 1 year. Bottle and store in a cool, dark place for up to 1 year more.

YIELD: ABOUT 2 CUPS (470 ML)

Variation: Many gentian (*Gentiana lutea*) species are endangered due to overharvesting and loss of habitat, so make sure you harvest or purchase it responsibly. As an alternative, you can replace the gentian with the roots of common "weeds" such as dandelion (*Taraxacum officinale*) and burdock (*Arctium lappa*). Although these roots still taste bitter, they're a bit milder and sweeter than gentian.

Calendula Sunshine Bitters

BARTENDER NEYAH WHITE'S RECIPE FOR SUNSHINE BITTERS, FEATURED in Molly Wellmann's *Handcrafted Cocktails*, calls for saffron and cardamom. I was inspired to create a version of these bitters using calendula flowers (*Calendula officinalis*), which, if you ask me, are pure sunshine. (They're also quite a bit less expensive than saffron, happily!) The calendula petals lend the bitters a golden color and a slightly bitter, peppery flavor, while the peel and pith of oranges impart a bright, citrusy note. You can use these in the same way you'd use any type of cocktail bitters—although I like to showcase them in a glass of sparkling water or a flute of Prosecco.

2 medium oranges

¼ cup (4 g) dried calendula petals or ½ cup (36 g) fresh, separated from sepals

2 tablespoons (10 g) green cardamom pods, cracked

2 cups (470 ml) vodka

Peel the oranges by hand, separating the fruit from the white pith and skin. Reserve the naked fruits for another use. Chop the pith and skin into pea-size pieces.

Combine the orange pieces, calendula petals, and cardamom pods in a pint (470 ml) jar. Pour the vodka into the jar. Cap the jar tightly. Store it in a cool, dark place for 1 week, shaking daily.

Strain the mixture through a fine-mesh strainer lined with a coffee filter or flour sack cloth; discard the solids. Bottle and store in a cool, dark place for up to 1 year.

YIELD: ABOUT 2 CUPS (470 ML)

Elderberry Elixir

THANKS TO THE ELDERBERRIES, ROSE HIPS, AND ORANGE PEELS, THIS warming, immune-boosting elixir packs a serious wallop of vitamin C—and it may also shorten the severity or duration of a cold or flu when taken by the ½ teaspoon every few hours. Elixirs are a great way to enjoy brandy, often changing doubters' minds about the spirit. To serve, pour ½ to 1 ounce (15 to 30 ml) into a shot glass and enjoy it neat or in a hot toddy.

3 cups (435 g) fresh elderberries or 1½ cups (218 g) dried

¼ cup (20 g) dried, cut, and sifted rose hips or ½ cup (100 g) fresh

Peel of 2 medium oranges, cut in wide strips, or 2 tablespoons (12 g)
  dried, cut, and sifted orange peel

2 whole cloves

⅔ cup (224 g) honey

2 cups (470 ml) brandy, or more if needed

3-inch (7.5 cm) cinnamon stick

Combine the elderberries, rose hips, orange peel, and cloves in a quart (1 L) jar. Pour in the honey and stir well to coat the berries (a long-handled spoon or chopstick makes a good stirring tool). Gradually add the brandy, stirring to moisten the ingredients and release air bubbles. If necessary, add a bit more brandy to cover the ingredients. Tuck the cinnamon stick under the liquid.

Wipe the rim of the jar with a clean, damp cloth and cap the jar tightly. Store it in a cool, dark place for 1 to 2 months, shaking occasionally and making sure the ingredients stay submerged. Strain the mixture through a fine-mesh strainer lined with a fine-mesh bag or flour sack cloth, squeezing to extract all of the liquid. Discard the solids. Bottle and store in a cool, dark place for up to 1 year.

YIELD: ABOUT 2 CUPS (470 ML)

Apricot and Meadowsweet Liqueur

FRESH APRICOTS CAN BE HIT OR MISS: EITHER THEY'RE PERFECT, HONEYED bliss, or they're dry, mealy disappointments. Fortunately, as long as they have good flavor, even apricots with less-than-perfect textures can be used to make tasty liqueurs. Meadowsweet flowers, which have a delicate, almond-like aroma, provide a nice complement. What's more, aspirin was originally derived from meadowsweet (*Filipendula ulmaria*), which contains salicylic acid. I don't know whether this liqueur will cure an ornery headache, but it sure can cheer you up! (If you can't get ahold of fresh apricots, you can also make this liqueur from dried ones, although the taste won't be quite as vibrant.)

2 tablespoons (2 g) fresh meadowsweet flowers or 1 tablespoon (2 g) dried

1 pound (454 g) fresh apricots

1 bottle (750 ml, or 3¼ cups) vodka

1 cup (235 ml) Simple Syrup (page 51)

Shake the meadowsweet flowers to remove any dirt or insects. Separate the flowers from the stems. Pit and chop the apricots. Combine the meadowsweet flowers and apricots in a quart (1 L) jar. Pour the vodka into the jar, making sure the fruit and flowers are submerged. Cap the jar tightly. Store it in a cool, dark place for 2 weeks, shaking daily and making sure the fruit and flowers stay submerged. Strain the mixture through a fine-mesh strainer lined with a coffee filter or flour sack cloth; discard the solids.

Pour the liquor and Simple Syrup into a clean jar, cover, and shake to combine. Age for at least 1 week. Bottle and store in a cool, dark place for up to 1 year.

YIELD: ABOUT 1 QUART (940 ML)

> **Variation:** Replace the apricots with loquats (*Eriobotrya japonica*); depending on the species, they may taste like a combination of apricot, plum, pear, or lychee. In this variation, the meadowsweet is optional.

Crème de Mûre

BLACKBERRY LIQUEUR, KNOWN AS *CRÈME DE MÛRE* IN FRANCE, CAN be made with different spirits, including vodka, brandy, and even whiskey. I like to use a combination of vodka and brandy because the result is a liqueur that's straightforward enough to use in a wide range of drinks (such as a bramble, Kir royale, or mint julep), but that has a little extra richness thanks to the brandy. Turn this recipe into *crème de cassis* by replacing the blackberries with black currants, or use red currants, elderberries, or huckleberries (*Gaylussacia baccata, Vaccinium parvifolium*).

3 cups (435 g) blackberries
¾ cup (180 ml) brandy
1½ cups (355 ml) vodka, or more if needed
1 cup (235 ml) Simple Syrup (page 51)

Place the blackberries in a bowl and lightly crush them using a potato masher or a fork. Transfer the blackberries and their juices to a quart (1 L) jar. Pour the brandy and vodka into the jar, making sure the blackberries are completely submerged; if necessary, add a bit more vodka to cover them.

Cap the jar tightly. Store it in a cool, dark place for at least 2 months, shaking occasionally and making sure the blackberries stay submerged. Strain the mixture through a fine-mesh strainer lined with a coffee filter or flour sack cloth. Discard the solids. Combine the liquor and Simple Syrup in a clean jar. Age it for at least 1 month, but ideally for several months. Bottle and store in a cool, dark place for up to 1 year.

YIELD: ABOUT 1 QUART (940 ML)

Hawthorn and Rose Elixir

ALTHOUGH HAWTHORN TREES DON'T GROW IN MY AREA, THEIR RED BERRIES are such a favorite of mine that I ask wildcrafter friends in other parts of the country to send me fresh ones every autumn. (At other times of the year, I rely on the dried berries that are available from herb purveyors.) Hawthorn (*Crataegus monogyna*, *C. laevigata*) is often associated with both the physical and the emotional heart, and I think this elixir is especially effective for afflictions of the latter. Along with rose, it's a great ally, providing courage in times of stress or change. Take little spoonfuls of this delicious tonic when you're in the process of making personal or professional leaps—or during the seasonal shift from summer to autumn, when the days shorten and spirits begin to droop. (Note: Avoid ingesting hawthorn seeds, which contain cyanide-inducing glycosides.)

2½ cups (500 g) fresh hawthorn berries or 1½ cups (180 g) dried

½ cup (6 g) dried rose petals or 1 cup fresh (30 g)

2 green cardamom pods, cracked

½ cup (170 g) honey

⅔ cup (160 ml) port wine

1⅓ cups (313 ml) brandy, or more if needed

3-inch (7.5 cm) cinnamon stick

1 vanilla bean, split

Combine the hawthorn berries, rose petals, and cardamom in a quart (1 L) jar. Pour in the honey and stir well to coat the hawthorn and rose (a long-handled spoon or chopstick makes a good stirring tool). Stir in the wine. Gradually add the brandy, stirring to moisten the ingredients and release air bubbles. If necessary, add a bit more brandy to cover the ingredients. Tuck the cinnamon stick and vanilla bean under the liquid.

Wipe the rim of the jar with a clean, damp cloth and cap the jar tightly. Store it in a cool, dark place for 1 to 2 months, shaking occasionally and making sure the ingredients stay submerged. Strain the mixture through a fine-mesh strainer lined with a fine-mesh bag or flour sack cloth, squeezing to extract all of the liquid. Discard the solids. Bottle and store in a cool, dark place for up to 1 year.

YIELD: ABOUT 2 CUPS (470 ML)

INFUSIONS, BITTERS, AND LIQUEURS

Douglas Fir Liqueur

IN SPRING, DOUGLAS FIR TIPS ARE BRIGHT GREEN WITH A CRISP, LEMONY flavor, and as the year progresses, the needles become more and more aromatic. You can make this liqueur with Douglas fir needles at any time of year, but I usually reserve the young tips for teas and syrups, such as the Pine Syrup on page 62, and use the more resinous autumn needles for an infusion that combines sweet hawthorn (*Crataegus monogyna, C. laevigata*) berries and warm allspice, like this one. Pine (*Pinus* spp.), spruce (*Picea* spp.), or white fir (*Abies concolor*) will all work well in place of Douglas fir (*Pseudotsuga menziesii*), too. Try it with gin cocktails, such as a gimlet, to amp up the foresty feel, or pair it with whiskey or bourbon-based cocktails, like a Manhattan, to enhance its warmth.

2 large handfuls conifer tips or needles, roughly chopped

½ cup (60 g) dried hawthorn berries or 1 cup (100 g) fresh

2 whole allspice berries

1 bottle (750 ml, or 3¼ cups) vodka

1 cup (235 ml) Simple Syrup (page 51)

Combine the chopped conifer, hawthorn berries, and allspice in a quart (1 L) jar. Pour the vodka into the jar, making sure the ingredients are completely submerged. Cap the jar tightly. Store it in a cool, dark place for 1 to 2 weeks, shaking daily.

Strain the mixture through a fine-mesh strainer lined with a coffee filter or flour sack cloth. Stir in the Simple Syrup. Age for at least 1 week, then bottle and store in a cool, dark place for up to 1 year.

YIELD: ABOUT 1 QUART (940 ML)

Fig and Vanilla Rum

WHEN I WAS A KID, MY MOTHER AND I USED TO WALK PAST TWO FRUIT trees on our way to school: a mulberry and a fig. I preferred the sweet berries, so I was puzzled by my mother's interest in the figs. Years later, I realized that Mom knew what was up: a wild fig tree is a precious friend! If there are no fig trees in your local area, though, don't despair. This Black Mission fig- and vanilla-infused rum can be made with either fresh or dried fruit. The rich liquor can be sipped neat or used in cocktails such as a rum old-fashioned or swizzle. You can also use it to spike a cup of hot or iced coffee, or to drizzle over desserts like ice cream or bread pudding.

1 pound (454 g) fresh or dried Black Mission figs, quartered

½ vanilla bean, split lengthwise

1 bottle (750 ml, or 3¼ cups) aged gold rum

Combine the figs and vanilla bean in a quart (1 L) jar. Pour the rum into the jar, making sure the figs are submerged. Cap the jar tightly. Store it in a cool, dark place for at least 1 month, shaking frequently and checking to make sure the figs stay submerged.

Strain the mixture through a fine-mesh strainer lined with a coffee filter or flour sack cloth. (The figs probably won't have much flavor left in them, but go ahead and taste them, and if they're palatable, you can save them for another use—as a topping for ice cream, for instance.) Bottle and store in a cool, dark place for up to 1 year.

YIELD: ABOUT 3 CUPS (705 ML)

Lemon Balm Carmelite Water

CARMELITE WATER, ALSO KNOWN AS *EAU DE MÉLISSE DES CARMES*, IS
an herbaceous, slightly bitter lemon balm tonic that was created by a French
doctor in 1611. Distilled by Carmelite monks who grew the *mélisse*, or lemon balm
(*Melissa officinalis*), in their monastery gardens, it became a popular remedy for
headaches and anxiety, and was even used as a perfume. Although the original,
secret formula remains a mystery, historical accounts list lemon balm, angelica, and
aromatic spices like coriander and cinnamon among the ingredients. My version
of Carmelite water was inspired by a combination of old and new French recipes,
and I find that a few sips of it really do soothe frazzled nerves. It also makes a good
digestif, thanks to its combination of somewhat bitter and carminative, or gas-
relieving, herbs.

1½ cups (25 g) finely chopped dried lemon balm or 3 cups (75 g) fresh

1 tablespoon (4 g) finely chopped dried angelica root

1 tablespoon (5 g) coriander seeds

¼ teaspoon ground mace or nutmeg

4 whole cloves

3-inch (7.5 cm) cinnamon stick

Grated peel of 1 medium lemon (about 1 tablespoon, or 6 g)

1 bottle (750 ml, or 3¼ cups) vodka

1 cup (235 ml) Simple Syrup (page 51), or more to taste

If using fresh lemon balm, pat it with a clean, dry towel to remove any moisture. Combine
the lemon balm, angelica root, coriander seeds, mace, cloves, cinnamon stick, and lemon
peel in a quart (1 L) jar. Pour the vodka into the jar, stirring to moisten the lemon balm.
Cap the jar tightly. Store it in a cool, dark place for 2 weeks, shaking daily. Strain the
mixture through a fine-mesh strainer lined with a coffee filter or flour sack cloth. Discard
the solids.

Combine the liquor and Simple Syrup in a clean jar. Age it for at least 1 week. Taste and
sweeten it with more Simple Syrup, if desired. Bottle and store in a cool, dark place for up
to 1 year.

YIELD: ABOUT 1 QUART (940 ML)

Lemon Verbena Liqueur

EVER BURIED YOUR NOSE IN A BUNCH OF LEMON VERBENA AND LONGED to bottle its enticing, citrusy aroma? Well, here's how to do it! This fragrant liqueur was inspired by traditional French preparations for the herb, which has long been used to lift the spirits and aid digestion. Native to Argentina and Chile, lemon verbena was brought to Europe in the eighteenth century. These days, you're more likely to find it in a garden or farmers' market rather than a supermarket or in the wild. Fortunately, it's easy to grow as long as you have full sun. I cultivate it in a container on my apartment balcony. Chill this Lemon Verbena Liqueur and sip it neat, just as you would with limoncello, or use it to enliven a gin and tonic, a pitcher of lemonade, or a glass of fizzy water. For this recipe, you'll want to use fresh lemon verbena (*Aloysia citrodora*), which imparts a much brighter flavor and color than its dried counterpart.

40 fresh lemon verbena leaves

Peel of 1 medium lemon, cut in wide strips

1 bottle (750 ml, or 3¼ cups) vodka

About 2 cups (470 ml) Simple Syrup (page 51), to taste

Pat the lemon verbena leaves with a clean, dry towel to remove any moisture. Combine the lemon verbena, lemon peel, and vodka in a quart (1 L) jar. Cap the jar tightly. Store it in a cool, dark place for 2 weeks, shaking daily.

Strain the mixture through a fine-mesh strainer lined with a coffee filter or flour sack cloth; discard the solids. Combine the liquor and Simple Syrup to taste in a clean jar. Age for at least 1 week before drinking. Bottle and store in a cool, dark place for up to 1 year.

YIELD: ABOUT 1 QUART (940 ML)

INFUSIONS, BITTERS, AND LIQUEURS

Peach and Pecan Bourbon

THIS RECIPE IS A TRIBUTE TO MY HOME STATE OF TEXAS, WHERE I GREW up shelling pecans in my uncle Al and aunt Marydel's yard and picking sweet peaches in the Hill Country. A word of caution, though: infusing spirits with nuts can be tricky, because their skins contain tannins. Steep them for too long, and the liqueur can become bitter or astringent, but if you remove all the skins, the liqueur will be lacking in flavor. Taste the mixture frequently while it's steeping, and rely on your palate to know when the infusion is done.

3 medium peaches (1 pound, or 454 g)

2 tablespoons (30 g) brown sugar

1 bottle (750 ml, or 3¼ cups) good-quality bourbon

1 cup (8 ounces, or 224 g) raw shelled pecans

Chop the peaches and discard the pits. Combine the peaches, sugar, and bourbon in a quart (1 L) jar. Cap the jar tightly. Store it in a cool, dark place for 1 week, shaking it daily and making sure the peaches stay submerged.

After 1 week has passed, prepare the pecans. Soak the pecans in a bowl of water for 30 minutes. This will help remove any bitterness. Meanwhile, preheat the oven to 350°F (180°C, or gas mark 4) with a rack in the middle. Strain the pecans and pat them dry with a towel. Spread the pecans in an even layer on a rimmed baking sheet. Toast in the oven, stirring every few minutes, until aromatic and golden brown, about 10 minutes. Transfer the pecans to another baking sheet or a large plate and let cool to room temperature. Transfer the pecans to a food processor and pulse until finely chopped. (Or finely chop the pecans using a large knife.)

Add the pecans to the jar of peaches and bourbon. Store it in a cool, dark place for 3 to 7 days, shaking it daily and making sure the ingredients stay submerged. Taste often to determine when the pecan flavor tastes good to you. Strain through a fine-mesh strainer lined with a coffee filter or flour sack cloth. Discard the solids. Bottle and store in a cool, dark place for up to 1 year.

YIELD: ABOUT 3 CUPS (705 ML)

Kitchen Tip: Spirits infused with nuts will develop a layer of oil on top. Simply shake the bottle to redistribute the oil (and flavor) before serving. If you want to remove the oil for appearance's sake, freeze the spirit overnight or until the oil solidifies, then skim it off with a spoon.

Plum Gin

FOR THIS GIN-BASED LIQUEUR, I USE THE LITTLE ITALIAN PRUNE PLUMS
or French sugar plums (also known as *quetsche*) that appear at my farmers' market in
late summer and early fall, but you can use any type of cultivated plum, wild plum,
damson, or sloe. Keep in mind, though, that wild plum varieties are often more
astringent, so if you're using them, you may want to taste the liqueur after a month
and sweeten it with additional sugar. And there's no need to stick to gin alone:
you can also experiment with other spirits, such as vodka, whiskey, or even brandy.
Plum Gin can be served neat, over ice, or used to make a gin fizz.

1¼ pounds (568 g) plums

Peel of ½ lemon, cut in wide strips

½ cup (100 g) sugar, or more to taste

1 bottle (750 ml, or 3¼ cups) gin

Halve the plums. Remove and discard the pits. If the plums are larger than walnut size,
chop them into smaller pieces. Combine the plums, lemon zest, and sugar in a quart (1 L)
jar. Pour the gin into the jar, making sure the plums are completely submerged.

Cap the jar tightly. Store it in a cool, dark place for at least 2 months, shaking occasionally and making sure the plums stay submerged. The longer it infuses, the more complex
the flavor will be. After 1 month, you may want to taste the liqueur and sweeten with more
sugar, if desired. Strain the mixture through a fine-mesh strainer lined with a coffee filter
or flour sack cloth; discard the solids. Bottle and store in a cool, dark place for up to 1 year.
Age it for at least 1 month, but ideally several months, before drinking.

YIELD: ABOUT 3¹/₄ CUPS (750 ML)

Cherry Bounce

MY OBSESSION WITH CHERRY BOUNCE BEGAN WHEN I WAS GIFTED
20 pounds (9 kg) of fresh sweet cherries one summer. I made pies, I made shrubs, and, after researching a bunch of old recipes, I made cherry bounce. And putting up a jar (or three!) of this full-bodied, sweet liqueur has been a summer tradition ever since. We don't know exactly where and when cherry bounce originated, but we do know that Martha Washington had a recipe for it, and George Washington is reported to have carried a canteen of bounce with him on his travels. Over the centuries, cherry bounce has been made with both sweet cherries and sour ones, plus an array of spices and various spirits, such as brandy, rum, and whiskey. Here's my version.

1½ pounds (680 g) sweet cherries, pitted

4 whole allspice berries

2 whole cloves

¼ teaspoon ground mace or nutmeg

¾ cup (144 g) turbinado sugar

1 bottle (750 ml, or 3¼ cups) bourbon

Combine the cherries, allspice, cloves, mace, and sugar in a quart (1 L) jar. Pour the bourbon into the jar, making sure the cherries are submerged. Cap the jar tightly. Store it in a cool, dark place for at least 2 months, shaking occasionally. The longer it infuses, the better it will be. Strain the mixture through a fine-mesh strainer lined with a coffee filter or flour sack cloth, gently pressing on the cherries with the back of a spoon to squeeze out all the liquid. Discard the cherries, or reserve them for another use.

Bottle and store in a cool, dark place for up to 1 year.

YIELD: ABOUT 3 ¹/₂ CUPS (823 ML)

Mandarincello

LIMONCELLO IS PROBABLY THE BEST-KNOWN CITRUS LIQUEUR, BUT IT can be made with other citrus fruits, too, such as oranges, grapefruits, bergamots, pomelos, and kumquats. After I got what seemed like endless quantities of mandarin oranges in my CSA, I decided to put them to good use by making Mandarincello. Depending on the individual fruits, your Mandarincello may turn out to be orange or bright yellow. Either way, it's a crisp and refreshing liqueur, and, like limoncello, it makes a lovely after-dinner *digestivo*, as they say in Italian. (In China, too, the dried peels of mandarin oranges have long been used to aid digestion.) Mandarincello is simple to make, and it's delightfully flavorful, with health benefits to boot—so what's not to love? Serve it neat in small chilled glasses, or add a splash to soda water or sparkling wine.

10 to 15 mandarin oranges, such as satsumas or clementines
1 bottle (750 ml, or 3¼ cups) vodka
1 cup (235 ml) Simple Syrup (page 51), or more to taste

Peel the mandarins using a vegetable peeler, taking care to avoid as much of the bitter white pith as possible. If necessary, trim away any large pieces of pith with a paring knife. Reserve the flesh for another use. Place the peels in a quart (1 L) jar. Pour the vodka into the jar. Cap the jar tightly. Store it in a cool, dark place for 1 week, shaking it daily.

Strain the mixture into a bowl through a fine-mesh strainer lined with a coffee filter or flour sack cloth. Discard the solids. Stir in the Simple Syrup. Taste and sweeten with more syrup, if desired. Bottle and freeze for at least 1 day before serving. Store in the freezer for up to 3 months.

YIELD: ABOUT 1 QUART (940 ML)

CHAPTER 6

WINES AND PUNCHES

FROM THE WAY THEY SHOWCASE SEASONAL INGREDIENTS TO THEIR endless possibilities for creativity, wines steeped with fruits, herbs, and flowers encapsulate everything I love about handcrafted drinks. Typically served as an aperitif or to enliven festive occasions, these wines are nearly effortless to assemble, yet they're incredibly satisfying. And, although all of the recipes in this chapter fall into the category of infused wines, they're actually quite different from one another, from the French-style *vins maison* made from seasonal fruits to party-worthy punches and sangrias, and from herb- and spice-laden vermouths to hot, comforting mulled wines. What they all have in common, though, is that they begin with a bottle of red, white, or rosé wine, and then the wine is enhanced by the addition of botanicals, liquors, and sweeteners. (This process is often called fortifying and aromatizing the wine.)

And infused wines aren't just pretty faces, either. Long before folks were sipping them simply because they tasted good, they were using infused wines to preserve and administer medicine. That's because the alcohol in wine acts as a solvent that helps draw the medicinal properties and flavors out of plant material (although wine, due to its lower alcohol content, isn't as effective a preservative as spirits are). Medicated wines have been used in both Eastern and Western traditions. Since as early as 1250 BCE, for example, Chinese medical practitioners have infused wines with herbs like ginseng, walnuts, and angelica roots. The ancient Egyptians steeped herbs in wine, too: archaeologists have found traces of pine resin, rosemary, and sage in Egyptian wine-bearing vessels. Ancient Romans added spices like cardamom and saffron to their wine, as well as honey, and later, in medieval Europe, spiced wines were often called hippocras because the infusions were filtered through a conical sleeve invented by the Greek physician Hippocrates. Today, the spiced wine tradition continues in the form of Spanish sangria and in mulled wines like German glühwein, Nordic glögg, and English wassail.

Another fortified wine with a remarkable pedigree is vermouth, a seventeenth-century Italian medicinal wine. Today, we associate it with cocktails like martinis and Manhattans, but vermouth can also be sipped neat—my favorite way to appreciate a homemade version that's imbued with an array of carefully chosen roots, fruits, leaves, and flowers. The word *vermouth* comes from the German *wermut*, meaning "wormwood," and European law stipulates that vermouth must contain wormwood. Of course, at home we can feel free to experiment as much as we like. As a wildcrafter, I like to incorporate local cousins of wormwood, like common mugwort or even garden tarragon, into my homemade vermouth.

Whereas vermouth can incorporate up to dozens of botanicals, *vins maison* tend to be simpler affairs. The *vin maison*, or house wine, tradition comes from France, where homemade concoctions of wine, fruit, eau de vie, and sugar are typically served as aperitifs to stimulate the appetite before a meal. Popular *vins mason* highlight fleeting seasonal ingredients such as bitter oranges (*vin d'orange*), green walnuts (*vin de noix*), and sour cherries (*guignolet*), and each family develops its own unique recipe.

Crafting Infused Wines

WHEN YOU'RE CHOOSING A WINE FOR AN INFUSION, YOU DON'T NEED TO splurge on an expensive bottle. At the same time, herbs and spices won't magically transform a bad bottle of wine, so do pick something that you'd actually drink on its own. For white wine, a dry sauvignon blanc or pinot grigio is generally a good choice. For red wine, consider how dry or fruity you want the final result to be, and whether red berry–like flavors or dark fruit–like flavors will complement your ingredients. When it comes to rosé, I prefer dry French styles to sweet California rosé or zinfandel wines.

To help preserve the wine after the addition of fruits, herbs, and spices, you can also fortify your infused wine with liquor. Most wines clock in at around 11 to 14 percent alcohol by volume (ABV), and adding spirits increases the ABV to around 15 to 20 percent. Vodka is always a good, neutral choice, but depending on your ingredients, you might try brandy, rum, or any other spirit. I'm a fan of brandy, though: because it's also made from grapes, brandy can complement wine really well. I like the refinement a Cognac brandy lends; although it's a bit more expensive, you don't need too much, so even a small bottle will be enough to fortify many batches of wine. You might consider other types of eau de vie or fruit brandy, too, such as apple or pear.

What about sweeteners? Some of these recipes call for sugar or honey, which can help coax out the flavors of the infused wine and turn it into a tipple that's best for enjoying before or after dinner. Use any type of sweetener, but keep in mind that plain white sugar offers the most neutral flavor. Unrefined and brown sugars can overpower and discolor delicate wines and herbs. (Sometimes that's desirable, though. For instance, adding burnt sugar syrup to vermouth is essential: without it, the sweet vermouth just wouldn't be as rich and satisfying.)

One last caveat: start with small quantities, so that you can experiment without incurring too much expense or waste. Try making pint (470 ml) jars of mini-infusions over the course of a couple of days or weeks to get a sense of what you like, and then graduate to bigger batches after that. Most of the recipes in this chapter call for one bottle (750 ml, or 3 1/4 cups) of wine, but feel free to double, triple, or quadruple them: I've been known to infuse up to six bottles of my favorites! Finally, don't feel that you have to follow each of these recipes to the letter. Instead, use them as guides to the basic ratios of wine, spirit, sweetener, and botanicals, then get creative with the ingredients in your own backyard.

Rosemary Wine

ROSEMARY AND WINE HAVE BEEN PARTNERS FOR CENTURIES. ARCHAEO-logical evidence suggests that the ancient Egyptians infused wine with rosemary. In *Banckes' Herbal* of 1525, the author suggests that rosemary can "keep the wine from all sourness and evill savours." Also, rosemary has long been associated with memory, from the ancient Greek scholars who wore sprigs of the herb to improve concentration during exams to the early modern English who used it as a symbol of remembrance at weddings and funerals. And it's not all superstition, either: scientists have found that the smell of rosemary can increase memory by 75 percent. I can't promise that my Rosemary Wine will boost your memory—but I can tell you it makes a nice little aperitif, and that it's lovely as part of a white sangria.

3 (6-inch, or 15-cm) sprigs rosemary

3¼ cups (or a 750-milliliter bottle) dry white wine

Pat the rosemary with a clean, dry towel to remove any moisture. Gently bruise the rosemary by pressing on the leaves with a rolling pin (the side of a wine bottle also works) to help release their flavor.

Pour out 1 cup (235 ml) of the white wine and stuff the sprigs into the wine bottle. Using a funnel, pour as much of the cup of wine as possible back into the bottle, and make sure the rosemary sprigs are submerged.

Re-cork the bottle and store it in a cool, dark place for 1 to 2 weeks, checking to make sure that rosemary stays submerged. Strain through a fine-mesh strainer; discard the solids.

ABOUT 3 CUPS (705 ML)

Rose Petal Wine

ROSE WINE HAS BEEN AROUND AT LEAST SINCE ROMAN TIMES. IN *Apicius*, a collection of recipes from the late fourth or early fifth century, a recipe for *rosatum* called for sewing rose petals into a linen bag, steeping them in wine, and refreshing the petals every seven days for three weeks. The wine was then sweetened with honey. Sounds like a delicious recipe—although it was recommended for medicinal use as a laxative. My version is simpler, and, thankfully, far less potent! Use red or dark pink roses to infuse the wine with the prettiest dark-pink color.

2 cups (60 g) fresh rose petals or 1 cup (12 g) dried
¼ cup (60 ml) Cognac or Cognac-style brandy
1 bottle (750 ml, or 3¼ cups) dry white wine
¼ cup (85 g) mild honey

If using fresh rose petals, pat them with a clean, dry towel to remove any moisture. Put the petals in a quart (1 L) jar, and pour over the Cognac and wine. Cover the jar tightly and give it a good shake to combine. Refrigerate for 1 week. Strain the mixture through a fine-mesh strainer and discard the solids.

Put the strained wine and honey in a clean jar. Cover the jar tightly and give it a good shake. Age for at least 1 week more before serving. Serve chilled.

YIELD: ABOUT 3¹/₂ CUPS (825 ML)

Wildcrafting Tip: Whether you find them growing in the woods or your garden, all roses (*Rosa* spp.) are edible. However, you want to make sure of two things: one, that the roses are very fragrant; and two, that they are absolutely free of chemicals or pesticides. (For this reason, it's best to avoid store-bought roses, unless they're expressly sold for culinary use.)

Anise Hyssop and Peach Wine

A MEMBER OF THE MINT FAMILY THAT'S NATIVE TO THE GREAT PLAINS of North America, anise hyssop (*Agastache foeniculum*) has a sweet, aniseed flavor. Native Americans have valued its healing properties. The Cree traditionally included the flowers in medicine bundles, while the Cheyenne made anise hyssop tea to treat colds and the "dispirited heart." I love pairing anise hyssop with peach. Infused in rosé wine, they make a lovely aperitif for summer entertaining.

½ cup (8 g) fresh anise hyssop leaves or flowers or ¼ cup (4 g) dried

1 cup (170 g) pitted and chopped peaches (about 1 to 2 peaches)

3 tablespoons (60 g) mild honey

¼ cup (60 ml) vodka

1 bottle (750 ml, or 3¼ cups) dry rosé wine

If using fresh anise hyssop, pat it with a clean, dry towel to remove any moisture. Combine the anise hyssop, peaches, and honey in a quart (1 L) jar. Pour the vodka and wine into the jar, making sure the peaches and anise hyssop are submerged.

Cover the jar tightly. Refrigerate the jar for 2 to 4 weeks, shaking it occasionally. The longer it infuses, the stronger the flavor will be. Strain the mixture through a fine-mesh strainer. Discard the solids. Bottle and refrigerate for up to 1 month. Serve chilled.

YIELD: ABOUT 3 ¹/₂ CUPS (825 ML)

Wildcrafting Tip: Harvest anise hyssop leaves throughout the spring and summer growing seasons. Individual flowers may be plucked off the spikes, or you can clip off the entire flowering top of the plant. Anise hyssop is best when it's fresh, but, in a pinch, you can also use the dried version.

Raspberry Wine

ALTHOUGH INFUSED WINES ARE FREQUENTLY SERVED AS APERITIFS, here's one that makes a great after-dinner sipper. Flavored with raspberries and fortified with Cognac and Grand Marnier, it is rich with berry sweetness and a hint of bitter orange. I think of it as hypocras framboisé, or raspberry hippocras, after a raspberry wine recipe that appears in Jerry Thomas's *Bar-Tender's Guide* of 1862. His recipe for Hypocras Framboisé was made from a combination of raspberries, claret wine, high-proof alcohol, and powdered sugar. (Raspberry hippocras also appeared in eighteenth-century French housekeeping manuals, and may date back as far as the Middle Ages.) My version pairs especially well with rich chocolate cake, or, even easier, a square of fine dark chocolate. Of course, you can serve this sumptuous wine *as* dessert, too.

2 cups (12 ounces, or 340 g) raspberries

3 tablespoons (38 g) sugar

2 tablespoons (30 ml) Cognac or Cognac-style brandy

2 tablespoons (30 ml) Grand Marnier

1 bottle (750 ml, or 3¼ cups) red fruit-flavored red wine, such as pinot noir or Grenache

Combine the raspberries and sugar in a quart (1 L) jar and muddle them with the flat end of a rolling pin or a wooden spoon. Add the Cognac, Grand Marnier, and wine. Cover the jar tightly and shake it well.

Store the jar in a cool, dark place for 1 week, shaking it daily and ensuring the raspberries stay submerged. Strain the mixture through a fine-mesh strainer. Discard the solids. Bottle and consume within 1 month. Serve chilled or at room temperature.

YIELD: ABOUT 3 ½ CUPS (825 ML)

Apple and Sage Wine

THIS WINE WAS INSPIRED BY A RECIPE FOR WHITE WINE WITH HONEY and sage that appears in one of the oldest medieval cookbooks, *Tractatus de modo preparandi*. After experimenting with different base wines, I settled on moscato because its honeyed sweetness goes surprisingly well with the savory herb. As always, you won't need to break the bank when buying the wine for this infusion, because you'll be flavoring it. However, some budget-priced muscats can be cloyingly sweet, so choose a wine with a bit of crispness to it. You'll lose some of the *frizzante*, or fizz, in the infusing process, but that's okay: the result makes a lovely aperitif that's perfect for enjoying with friends in late summer or early fall.

1 medium apple

2 tablespoons (5 g) chopped fresh sage leaves

1 tablespoon (20 g) mild honey

¼ cup (60 ml) vodka

1 bottle (750 ml, or 3¼ cups) moscato d'Asti wine

Core and finely chop the apple, leaving the peel on. Combine the chopped apple, chopped sage, and honey in a quart (1 L) jar. Pour the vodka and wine into the jar, making sure the apples and sage are submerged.

Cover the jar tightly. Refrigerate the jar for 2 to 4 weeks, shaking it occasionally. The longer it infuses, the stronger the flavor will be. Strain through a fine-mesh strainer. Discard the solids. Bottle and store in the refrigerator for up to 1 month. Serve chilled.

YIELD: ABOUT 3¹/₂ CUPS (825 ML)

Vin de Noix

ALTHOUGH MOST PEOPLE ARE ONLY FAMILIAR WITH RIPE WALNUTS, you'll find green-walnut aficionados like me among the trees months before the main harvest, plucking the unripened nuts to make spectacular drinks. That includes the Italian-style *nocino* and this French-style *vin de noix*. Making my Vin de Noix is simple, but patience is one of the main ingredients. It's worth it, though: after several months of aging, the wine mellows into a luscious, spiced aperitif.

6 to 8 green walnuts, depending on size

Peel of ¼ medium orange, cut in wide strips

1-inch (2.5 cm) piece vanilla bean, split

1 small whole clove

½-inch (1.3 cm) piece cinnamon stick

½ cup (100 g) sugar, or more to taste

½ cup (120 ml) vodka

1 bottle (750 ml, or 3¼ cups) dry red wine

Rinse and dry the walnuts. Carefully cut the walnuts in half using a large, sturdy knife (I use a Chinese cleaver). Combine the walnuts, orange peel, vanilla, clove, cinnamon, and sugar in a sterilized quart (1 L) jar. Pour the vodka and wine into the jar, making sure the walnuts are submerged. Cover the jar tightly. Store in a cool, dark place for 1 month, shaking it daily.

Strain the mixture through a fine-mesh strainer lined with a coffee filter. Discard the solids. Sweeten with additional sugar, if desired. Bottle and store in a cool, dark place for up to 1 year. Age for at least 3 months before drinking. Vin de Noix will continue to improve with age. Serve in small glasses, chilled or at room temperature.

YIELD: ABOUT 1 QUART (940 ML)

 Wildcrafting Tip: Harvest green walnuts (*Juglans nigra, J. californica*) when the shells are soft enough to pierce. In Italy and France, that's usually done in June or July, but in my California home, I do it in May: any later and the shells would have hardened. If you can't find wild trees, ask a walnut farmer to harvest some nuts early. Then handle them with care: cut green walnuts can leave yellow stains on everything they touch. So use a cutting board that you won't mind staining, and either wear gloves or display your stained hands proudly as wildcrafting badges of honor.

May Wine

FIRST MENTIONED BY BENEDICTINE MONK WANDALBERT DE PRÜM IN 854, sweet woodruff-infused wine endures in Germany and Belgium, where it's enjoyed during May Day celebrations and at other seasonal festivals. There are many variations of May wine—also called Maiwein, Maitrank, Maibowle, and Wald-meisterbowle—involving different fruits, spices, and liqueurs. This one's my favorite, not least because it incorporates strawberries, another beloved sign of spring. If you don't have access to sweet woodruff (*Galium odoratum*), sweet clover (*Melilotus officinalis*) makes a good substitute. Both plants are more fragrant when dried. Dry them quickly and thoroughly to prevent mold or fermentation. Improperly dried herbs may contain high levels of blood-thinning chemicals.

¼ cup (50 g) sugar

¼ cup (60 ml) Cognac or Cognac-style brandy

1 bottle (750 ml, or 3¼ cups) semi-dry white wine
  (such as Moselle or Riesling), chilled

½ cup (10 g) dried sweet woodruff or sweet clover

Ice cubes

1 bottle (750 ml, or 3¼ cups) sparkling wine, chilled

½ cup (75 g) sliced strawberries, for garnish

Combine the sugar, brandy, and white wine in a pitcher or ½-gallon (2 L) jar and stir to dissolve the sugar. Stir in the sweet woodruff. Cover and refrigerate for 30 minutes to 2 hours (the longer it steeps, the stronger the flavor will be). Strain through a fine-mesh strainer. Discard the solids.

To serve, pour into ice-filled wine glasses or punch cups, and top with sparkling wine. Garnish with strawberries.

YIELD: ABOUT 6½ CUPS (1530 ML)

Botanical Note: High doses of sweet woodruff and sweet clover can cause headaches or dizziness due to the presence of an organic chemical compound called coumarin. Coumarin is responsible for the herbs' characteristic hay and vanilla aroma (it is also found in cassia cinnamon). So avoid over-steeping these herbs, and, as always, drink the wine in moderation.

Vin d'Orange

HERE'S A VITAL BIT OF KITCHEN (AND WILDCRAFTING) WISDOM: SOME recipes are meant to be enjoyed right away, while others are lovingly prepared for future pleasure. *Vin d'orange* falls into the latter category. Infused with winter citrus fruits, it reaches its prime in spring or summer—and that's when you'll thank yourself for having such foresight. (It's also when you'll lament that you didn't put up more!) Served as an aperitif, *vin d'orange* is traditionally made from bitter oranges and dry white or French-style rosé wine. Depending on where you live, bitter oranges may be hard to locate, so this version calls for more readily available navel oranges plus grapefruit. The result is a wine that's pleasantly bittersweet—delicious on its own over ice, or mixed with a little sparkling water.

2 large navel oranges (preferably Cara Cara)

1 small grapefruit (preferably white)

½ vanilla bean, split

½ cup (100 g) sugar

½ cup (120 ml) vodka

¼ cup (60 ml) brandy

1 bottle (750 ml, or 3¼ cups) dry white or dry rosé wine

Rinse and dry the oranges and grapefruit. Trim and discard the stem ends. Cut each orange into ¼-inch-thick (6 mm) rounds. Cut the grapefruit in half and then cut each half into ¼-inch-thick (6 mm) half-circles. Combine the oranges, grapefruit, vanilla, and sugar in a sterilized quart (1 L) jar. Pour the vodka, brandy, and wine into the jar and push the fruit down with a wooden spoon to submerge it as much as possible (it will insist on floating up). Cover the jar tightly. Store the jar in a cool, dark place for 1 month, shaking it daily to moisten the floating pieces of fruit with the alcohol mixture.

Strain through a fine-mesh strainer. Discard the solids. Bottle and store in the refrigerator for up to 6 months. Age for at least 1 month before drinking: the Vin d'Orange will continue to improve with age. Serve chilled.

YIELD: ABOUT 1 QUART (940 ML)

Variation: To use bitter oranges, replace the oranges and grapefruit with 3 Seville oranges.

Dry Vermouth

A TRADITIONAL EUROPEAN VERMOUTH WOULD CONTAIN WORMWOOD, BUT my Dry Vermouth calls upon wormwood's more accessible cousin: tarragon. Its slightly bittersweet, anise-like flavor lends the vermouth a delicate warmth, while hyssop—which has a long history of use in herbal beverages, like the liqueurs Bénédictine and Chartreuse—yields faint traces of licorice and mint. Though dry vermouths are typically associated with martinis, my favorite way to enjoy this one is pretty simple: in a small, ice-filled glass, with nothing more than a splash of soda and a twist of lemon.

Peel of 1 medium lemon, cut in wide strips

Peel of 1/4 grapefruit, cut in wide strips

1 tablespoon (4 g) finely chopped fresh tarragon

1 tablespoon (1 g) dried lemon balm

1 tablespoon (2 g) dried elderflowers

1 tablespoon (2 g) dried hyssop

1 tablespoon (0.75 g) dried rose petals

1 teaspoon dried chamomile flowers

1 teaspoon dried lavender flowers

1 bottle (750 ml, or 3 1/4 cups) dry white wine, divided

1/4 cup (60 ml) Simple Syrup (page 51)

1 cup plus 1 tablespoon (250 ml) Cognac or Cognac-style brandy

Combine the lemon peel, grapefruit peel, tarragon, lemon balm, elderflowers, hyssop, rose petals, chamomile flowers, lavender flowers, and 1 cup (235 ml) of the white wine in a medium saucepan. Bring to a boil over medium heat and then reduce the heat to low and simmer for 5 minutes. Remove from the heat and let cool. Strain the mixture through a fine-mesh strainer lined with a fine-mesh bag or flour sack cloth. Squeeze to extract all the liquid. Discard the solids.

Combine the strained wine and the remaining 2 1/4 cups (515 ml) white wine in a clean saucepan. Bring to a boil over medium heat and gradually add the Simple Syrup, stirring to combine. Remove from the heat and stir in the Cognac. Let cool completely.

Bottle and store in the refrigerator for up to 2 months. Age for at least 1 day before using.

YIELD: ABOUT 1 QUART (940 ML)

Sweet Vermouth

ALSO KNOWN AS RED VERMOUTH, SWEET VERMOUTH IS MADE WITH A white wine base that gets its color from caramelized sugar. I created this around several wildcrafted herbs, including mugwort, bee balm, sage, and California bay leaf. If they don't grow near you, play with your own local or dried herbs. Like other sweet vermouths, this one is delicious in cocktails like Manhattans or negronis.

½ cup (75 g) dried Black Mission figs, chopped

1 vanilla bean, split lengthwise and cut into 1-inch (2.5-cm) pieces

1 cup (235 ml) Armagnac or brandy

Peel of 1 medium orange, cut in wide strips

½ teaspoon dried bee balm, or ¼ teaspoon dried mint and ¼ teaspoon dried oregano

½ teaspoon dried mugwort

½ teaspoon dried sage

1 cinnamon stick

1 whole clove

2 whole star anise pods

½ dried California bay leaf or 1 dried Turkish bay leaf, torn into pieces

1 bottle (750 ml, or 3¼ cups) dry white wine, divided

¼ cup (60 ml) Burnt Sugar Syrup (page 53), more as needed

Combine the figs, vanilla bean, and Armagnac in a jar. Cover the jar tightly and store it in a cool, dark place for 2 days. Strain the mixture through a fine-mesh strainer. Discard the solids. Set aside in a covered jar.

Combine the orange peel, bee balm, mugwort, sage, cinnamon, clove, star anise, bay leaf, and 1 cup (235 ml) of the white wine in a saucepan. Bring to a boil over medium heat, and then reduce the heat to low and simmer for 5 minutes. Remove from the heat and let cool. Strain the mixture through a fine-mesh strainer lined with a fine-mesh bag or flour sack cloth. Squeeze to extract all the liquid. Discard the solids.

Combine the strained wine and the remaining 2¼ cups (515 ml) white wine in a medium saucepan. Bring to a boil over medium heat and gradually add the Burnt Sugar Syrup, stirring to combine. Remove from the heat and stir in the reserved Armagnac. Let cool. Taste and sweeten with additional Burnt Sugar Syrup, if desired. Bottle and store in the refrigerator for up to 2 months. Age for at least 1 day before using.

YIELD: ABOUT 1 QUART (940 ML)

Claret Cup

"THE LEAVES AND FLOURES OF BORAGE PUT INTO WINE MAKE MEN AND women glad and merry and drive away all sadnesse, dulnesse and melancholy," wrote sixteenth-century herbalist John Gerard. With its brilliant blue flowers and cucumber-like flavor, borage (*Borago officinalis*) has enhanced wine for centuries, even millennia. Roman and Celtic warriors drank borage-steeped wine for courage, while the Victorians used borage to garnish the claret cup, a popular punch made with red wine from Bordeaux plus various liqueurs, herbs, fruits, and spices. (Pimm's Cup, which also traditionally includes borage, may have originated as a variation of the claret cup.) This is my version of a claret cup, and it's inspired by recipes in historical cookbooks. The first delicious step involves creating a fragrant blend of lemon oil and sugar called *oleo-saccharum*, a classic technique for adding depth of flavor to punches.

Peel of 1 medium lemon, cut in wide strips

¼ cup (50 g) sugar

1 borage sprig, plus flowers for garnish

¼ cup (60 ml) pale, dry sherry (such as fino)

1 bottle (750 ml, or 3¼ cups) dry red wine (such as Bordeaux), chilled

Ice cubes

1 bottle (940 ml, or 1 quart) club soda, chilled

Combine the lemon peels and sugar in a bowl. Using a muddler or the back of a wooden spoon, muddle the lemon peels and sugar until the peels start to release their oils. Let stand for 30 minutes.

Combine the lemon peel and sugar mixture in a clean pitcher with the borage sprig, sherry, and red wine. Stir to combine. Cover and refrigerate for 1 hour. Strain through a fine-mesh strainer. Discard the solids.

To serve, pour into ice-filled glasses and top with club soda. Garnish with borage flowers.

YIELD: ABOUT ½ GALLON (2 L)

Kumquat and Mint Sangria

EVERY WINTER, I WAIT FOR MY FRIEND JENNY TO CALL WITH THE GOOD
news: *The kumquats are ripe!* That's when I hop on a bus and head over to her
mom's backyard in Koreatown, where I get out the ladder and harvest to my heart's
content. Although they look like miniature oranges, kumquats are unique members
of the citrus family—their skin is sweet while their flesh is tart. In Chinese New Year
celebrations, kumquats symbolize good luck and prosperity. I love the way they
seem to make everything bright and sunny, whether it's a jar of kumquat marma-
lade or a refreshing glass of Kumquat and Mint Sangria.

2 tablespoons (30 ml) Simple Syrup (page 51) or sugar (25 g)

¼ cup (60 ml) orange liqueur, such as Cointreau

1 bottle (750 ml, or 3¼ cups) crisp white wine,
   such as pinot grigio or Riesling

10 kumquats, thinly sliced and seeded

1 orange, thinly sliced and seeded

½ cup (48 g) fresh mint leaves

Ice cubes

Combine the Simple Syrup, orange liqueur, and wine in a pitcher or ½-gallon (2 L) jar and
stir to dissolve the sugar. Stir in the kumquats, sliced orange, and mint. Cover and refrigerate for 1 hour. To serve, pour into ice-filled glasses, and watch your guests swoon.

YIELD: ABOUT 3 ½ CUPS (825 ML)

Mulled Wine

LACED WITH PINK PEPPER AND FENNEL SEEDS, THIS SWEET AND FRUITY
mulled wine offers a change of pace from the heavily spiced versions many of us
are familiar with. For me, mulled wine is a potable celebration of my local flora, fea-
turing clementines from my CSA box; fennel seeds and bay leaves I gathered on a
coastal hike; and pink peppercorns from the tree next door. Depending on where
you live, you might want to invent your own unique version of mulled wine, using
ingredients like juniper berries, sage leaves, elderberries, maple syrup, local honey,
or a splash of homemade liqueur. Feel free to use whatever looks good to you.
(Note: Avoid pink peppercorns if you are allergic to cashews or tree nuts.)

6 mandarin oranges

2 dried California bay leaves or 4 dried Turkish bay leaves,
  folded in half down the center vein

2 (3-inch, or 7.5 cm) cinnamon sticks

2 teaspoons fennel seeds

2 teaspoons pink peppercorns, lightly crushed

⅔ cup brown sugar (150 g) or honey (224 g), or to taste

2 bottles (750 ml, or 3¼ cups each) fruity red wine, divided

Using a vegetable peeler, peel the oranges in wide strips. Squeeze the juice from the
oranges. Combine the orange peels and juice, bay leaves, cinnamon sticks, fennel seeds,
pink peppercorns, brown sugar, and 1 cup (235 ml) of the red wine in a large pot. Simmer
over medium heat, stirring to dissolve the sugar. Continue to simmer, stirring occasionally, for 5 minutes.

Stir in the remaining 5½ cups (1265 ml) red wine. Gently simmer (but do not boil)
until the mixture is warmed through. Strain through a fine-mesh strainer. Discard the
solids. Serve warm.

YIELD: ABOUT 6½ CUPS (1500 ML)

CHAPTER 7

FIZZY FERMENTATIONS

S ODAS WERE SOME OF THE FIRST WILD DRINKS I EVER MADE, WHICH is funny, because I didn't even like soda at the time. But I was searching for new ways to use foraged ingredients, and plus, I wanted to dream up new flavor combinations for my soda-loving husband. Along the way, I discovered sodas that I enjoyed, too. I also became interested in traditional sodas, which encompass both wild ingredients and health benefits. Take dandelion and burdock, for instance, a classic soda that's made from roots dug up in the wild and turned into a tonic to support liver health. And that's just one example. Before mass-produced sodas became the sugary villains they are today, sodas were regularly consumed for health reasons as well as for pleasure, and soda fountains themselves were situated right inside pharmacies. These days, handmade sodas can still be good for you. Some sodas, such as those made from water kefir grains and "ginger bugs," even contain probiotics that can support healthy digestion. (Sounds good to me: I know I'd much rather get my probiotics from naturally fermented foods and drinks than from a pill!)

So, when it comes to soft drinks, there's no need to limit yourself to the artificially flavored and high-fructose-corn-syrup-filled stuff you find in grocery stores. There are infinite ways to customize your homemade sodas, and it's easy to tailor your fizzy drinks to your palate—and to the particular season, time, and place in which you live.

Crafting Fizzy Fermented Drinks

IT'S MY HOPE THAT THE RECIPES IN THIS CHAPTER ARE USER-FRIENDLY enough for the fermentation beginner, yet interesting enough for the more seasoned brewer. All of the projects here require a minimum investment of equipment and time, so that you can look forward to sipping your sodas within a week or so. And once you get a feel for the recipes, you'll be able to adapt them to showcase any fruits, herbs, and spices you like. But first, let's run through the main ingredients in fizzy fermented drinks.

YEAST

Yeast is essential to the fermentation of sweet liquids, because it is what converts sugar into ethanol, creating carbon dioxide (read: bubbles). The presence of ethanol means that every fermented drink has a trace amount of alcohol, typically less than 1 percent. However, the alcohol level depends on factors such as the amount of sugar and duration of fermentation. To measure specific alcohol content, use a tool called a hydrometer, which can be purchased in home-brewing stores. (Although you should use your own judgment, most of these sodas clock in at around 0.5 percent ABV, and many people are comfortable with serving them to children. That said, you may wish to taste your beverages and check alcohol levels before serving them to kids.)

What kind of yeast should you use for your handcrafted sodas? That, for the most part, is completely up to you. In keeping with the wild theme, you might harness the yeasts that exist naturally in the environment and on the surfaces of fruits and roots like ginger. Or you might call upon a specific, commercial strain of yeast, such as those that are cultivated for making Champagne and ale. (You can even use bread yeast in a pinch, but the flavor won't be quite as nice.) There are pros and cons to each method, and most of the soda recipes in this chapter include both options. Cultivated yeasts ensure a more consistent result, while wild yeasts have that (alluring!) wild-card factor: you can never be entirely sure how they'll ferment, or what the end result will taste like. Plus, the wild yeast method in this chapter relies on ginger, which will give all sodas a light ginger flavor.

In addition to the wild yeast or "ginger bug" and cultivated yeast sodas, this chapter includes sodas made with water kefir, a symbiotic colony of bacteria and yeast (SCOBY). (If you've ever had kombucha, you're already familiar with a type of SCOBY.) Although they're called "grains," water kefir grains look more like gelatinous blobs (and they contain no actual grains or gluten). The grains must be purchased or obtained from a friend at the outset, but if you take good care of them, they'll multiply and can be used to create infinite batches of soda. Water kefir is mild in flavor, and I go for sodas that are made from it when I want a drink that's less sweet and sometimes more herbal in nature.

To prevent cross-contamination, keep different types of cultures 4 to 6 feet (1.2 to 1.8 m) apart from each other when they're not covered with lids (if, for instance, they're only covered with a coffee filter or a piece of cloth). So, if you're making, say, a ginger bug and water kefir (or other ferments like sourdough or kombucha) at the same time, you might want to store them on opposite sides of the kitchen, or even in different rooms.

WATER

CHLORINE CAN DESTROY YEAST and bacteria, so either use filtered water or springwater, or leave chlorinated tap water out on the countertop for 24 hours to let the chlorine in it evaporate. But avoid distilled water: it lacks minerals that are necessary for fermentation.

SUGAR

YEASTS NEED TO EAT SUGAR TO survive. Without it, you wouldn't be able to make a fermented and fizzy beverage. For the ginger bug and Champagne yeast sodas, you'll generally need at least 1 to 2 tablespoons (12.5 to 25 g) of sugar to feed the yeast. The recipes in this chapter usually call for more than that, though, so that the soda will be sweet and palatable. If you like, reduce the amount of sugar, or make up the difference with another type of sweetener. For water kefir, most of the sugar is involved in the initial fermentation. In the second fermentation, to make soda, you might want to add a little sugar—in the form of granulated sugar or fruit—to create a fizzier drink.

CONTAINERS

JARS AND BOTTLES SHOULD BE VERY CLEAN—AT THE VERY LEAST, THOROUGHLY washed with hot water and soap. You can also sanitize jars and bottles—see page 19 to find out how—to prevent the growth of unwanted microorganisms and off-flavors.

The recipes in this chapter make 1 quart (1 L) or ½ gallon (2 L) of soda. The number of bottles you'll need depends on the size of your bottles.

BOTTLE SIZE	BOTTLES PER QUART (1 L)	BOTTLES PER ½ GALLON (2 L)
2 liter (2 quarts)	Do not use	1 bottle
1 liter (1 quart)	1 bottle	2 bottles
½ liter (1 pint)	2 bottles	4 bottles
32 ounce (1 L)	1 bottle	2 bottles
16 ounce (½ L)	2 bottles	4 bottles

Because of the pressure that builds up from carbonation, there's always a risk that bottles might explode. If you are new to making sodas or other fermented drinks, I strongly recommend that you do all your bottling in plastic bottles. If you're using a plastic bottle, you'll know your soda is carbonated and ready if the bottle feels firm when squeezed. (You can also open the bottle occasionally to sample the soda and test for fizziness.) If you do use glass bottles, use swing-top, Grolsch-style bottles that are meant for carbonation. Carefully open or "burp" the bottles several times a day to release excess gases.

One last word: It's a good idea to open homemade soda bottles over the sink, because they can be very fizzy!

Ginger Bug Soda Starter

MAKING YOUR OWN NATURALLY CARBONATED SODAS IS EASY WHEN YOU use this wild yeast soda starter, also known as a ginger bug. Similar to a sourdough starter, a slurry of ginger, sugar, and water helps capture wild yeast, and provides an environment for lactic acid bacteria (the good guys!) to flourish. Sugar is necessary, because it feeds the bacteria and yeast (some people use honey, but that can take several weeks longer). I typically use a raw or unrefined sugar, but plain white sugar can work, too. Once the starter culture is ready, it can be added to tea or juice to make a soda. You can also replenish the starter to keep it alive and continue to make new batches of soda. Use organically grown ginger: nonorganic ginger may have undergone irradiation, which can destroy the good yeast and bacteria.

Unpeeled, organically grown ginger

Sugar

Water

Combine 2 tablespoons (12 g) finely chopped or grated ginger, 2 tablespoons (25 g) sugar, and 1/4 cup (60 ml) water in a pint (470 ml) jar. Cover the jar with a coffee filter or a piece of cloth secured with a rubber band. Let the jar stand at warm room temperature, out of direct sunlight.

The next day, stir in 2 tablespoons each ginger (12 g), sugar (25 g), and water (30 ml). Repeat this process daily for up to a week. The starter is ready when it is foamy or bubbly around the top and smells mildly yeasty. Depending on the temperature of your environment, it may take from 2 to 7 days. (If nothing has happened in 7 days, discard it and start over again.)

To use the starter: Strain off 1/2 cup (120 ml) liquid and combine with 2 quarts (2 L) juice or tea (for full instructions, see the Ginger Bug Soda recipe on page 163). Replenish the starter, if desired.

To replenish the starter: Remove half of the sediment from the jar. Add 1/4 cup (60 ml) water, 2 tablespoons (12 g) ginger, and 2 tablespoons (25 g) sugar to the jar and gently stir. Continue to feed it daily as described above until it is bubbly again.

To store the starter: Refrigerate the starter in a closed jar and feed it 2 tablespoons each ginger (12 g), sugar (25 g), and water (30 ml) once a week. To reactivate it, let it reach room temperature and continue to feed it daily until it is bubbly again.

Ginger Bug Soda

SODAS MADE WITH A GINGER BUG HAVE A SLIGHT, THOUGH NOT OVER-whelming, gingery taste, so use a juice or tea that complements ginger. The flavor can also vary depending on the wild yeasts in your environment, making each batch of soda totally unique.

½ gallon (2 L) fruit juice or strong tea (see chapter 2)

About ½ cup (100 g) sugar (or another caloric sweetener, such as honey or agave nectar)

¼ cup (60 ml) strained liquid from Ginger Bug Soda Starter (page 162)

Sweeten the juice with the sugar. It should be quite sweet, because the yeast will need to consume the sugar to create carbonation. If the juice or tea has been heated, cool it to room temperature.

Combine the sweetened juice and starter liquid in a jar and stir to blend. Cover the jar with a coffee filter or a piece of cloth and secure it with a rubber band.

Bubbles should form on the top within 1 to 3 days. Once it is bubbly, transfer the soda to a bottle. Store the bottle at room temperature for 1 to 5 days until the soda is sufficiently carbonated. Transfer the bottle to the refrigerator and drink within 2 weeks.

YIELD: ABOUT ½ GALLON (2 L)

Ginger Ale

NEVER FEAR: THIS RECIPE ISN'T JUST FOR GINGER ALE FANS. IT'S ALSO an example of how you can use this basic template with any of the syrups featured in chapter 3, or with another syrup of your own invention. If you're using this as a template for other sodas, the lemon juice called for is optional.

CHAMPAGNE YEAST FERMENTATION

1 recipe Ginger Syrup (page 54)

1 to 2 tablespoons (6 to 12 g) grated fresh ginger (optional)

Juice of 1 medium lemon (optional, see headnote)

About 7 cups (1645 ml) lukewarm, unchlorinated water

⅛ teaspoon Champagne yeast

Using a funnel, pour the Ginger Syrup into a ½-gallon (2 L) bottle. Add the fresh ginger and lemon juice. Top off the bottle with the water, leaving at least 1 inch (2.5 cm) of headspace. Add the yeast to the bottle. Cap the bottle tightly and shake it well. Store the bottle at room temperature, out of direct sunlight, for 1 to 3 days. When the soda is carbonated (see page 161), transfer the bottle to the refrigerator. Store in the refrigerator and drink within 2 weeks.

YIELD: ½ GALLON (2 L)

GINGER BUG FERMENTATION

GINGER ALE MADE WITH A GINGER BUG HAS DOUBLE THE HEALTH BEN-
efits: the natural probiotics in the ginger bug can aid digestion and support the
immune system, too.

1 recipe Ginger Syrup (page 54)

1 tablespoon (6 g) grated fresh ginger (optional)

Juice of 1 medium lemon (about 2 tablespoons, or 30 ml)

1 cup (235 ml) strained liquid from Ginger Bug Soda Starter (page 162)

About 6 cups (1410 ml) lukewarm, unchlorinated water

Combine the Ginger Syrup, fresh ginger, lemon juice, and Ginger Bug Soda Starter in a wide-mouth, ¹/₂-gallon (2 L) jar. Top off the jar with the water, leaving 1 inch (2.5 cm) of headspace. Give it a good stir. Cover the jar with a coffee filter or a piece of cloth secured with a rubber band.

Let the jar stand at warm room temperature, out of direct sunlight. You should start to see bubbles forming on the top within 1 to 5 days, depending on the temperature of your environment and the wild yeasts present.

Once the mixture is bubbly, stir it. Then, using a funnel, pour it into a bottle, leaving at least 1 inch (2.5 cm) of headspace. Cap the bottle and store it at room temperature for 1 to 5 days. When the soda is carbonated (see page 161), transfer the bottle to the refrigerator. Store in the refrigerator and drink within 2 weeks.

YIELD: ¹/₂ **GALLON (2 L)**

Dandelion and Burdock

AS EARLY AS THE THIRTEENTH CENTURY, HERBALISTS AND HOME COOKS relied on the classic combination of dandelion and burdock to support liver and kidney health. This recipe uses ground dandelion and burdock roots. To grind dried pieces of root, process them in a coffee grinder, spice grinder, or mortar and pestle. For sweetening, I prefer plain white sugar; however, you can also use an unrefined sugar such as turbinado or jaggery.

DANDELION AND BURDOCK SODA BASE

2 tablespoons (½ ounce, or 14 g) coarsely ground dried dandelion root

2 tablespoons (½ ounce, or 14 g) coarsely ground dried burdock root

½-inch (1.3 cm) piece fresh ginger, grated (1½ teaspoons)

Grated peel of ½ medium lemon (1½ teaspoons)

1 whole star anise pod

1½ cups (355 ml) water

1 cup (100 g) sugar

Juice of 1 medium lemon (2 tablespoons, or 30 ml)

Combine the dandelion, burdock, ginger, lemon peel, star anise, and water in a saucepan. Cover and bring to a boil. Reduce the heat to low and simmer, covered, for 20 minutes. Strain through a fine-mesh strainer, pressing with the back of a spoon to extract all the liquid. Discard the solids. Stir in the sugar and lemon juice. Let cool to room temperature. Follow the instructions below to make soda using either Champagne yeast or a ginger bug.

CHAMPAGNE YEAST FERMENTATION

DANDELION AND BURDOCK SODA, OR "D&B," AS WE CALL IT IN OUR HOUSE, tastes like a mild root beer—slightly earthy and very refreshing when served over ice.

1 recipe Dandelion and Burdock Soda Base (above)

About 7 cups (1645 ml) lukewarm, unchlorinated water

⅛ teaspoon Champagne yeast

Using a funnel, pour the Dandelion and Burdock Soda Base into a bottle. Top off the bottle with the lukewarm water, leaving at least 1 inch (2.5 cm) of headspace. Add the yeast to the bottle. Cap the bottle tightly and shake it well.

Store the bottle at room temperature, out of direct sunlight, for 1 to 3 days. When the soda is carbonated (see page 161), transfer the bottle to the refrigerator. Store in the refrigerator and drink within 2 weeks.

YIELD: 1/2 GALLON (2 L)

GINGER BUG FERMENTATION

DIGESTIVE BENEFITS ABOUND WHEN YOU MAKE THIS WITH A GINGER BUG. In addition to the probiotics in the soda starter, dandelion and burdock roots contain a starch called inulin, which acts as a prebiotic (food for beneficial probiotics).

1 recipe Dandelion and Burdock Soda Base (page 166)

1 cup (235 ml) strained liquid from Ginger Bug Soda Starter (page 162)

About 6 cups (1410 ml) lukewarm, unchlorinated water

Combine the Dandelion and Burdock Soda Base and strained Ginger Bug Soda Starter in a wide-mouth, 1/2-gallon (2 L) jar. Top off the jar with the lukewarm water, leaving 1 inch (2.5 cm) of headspace. Give it a good stir. Cover the jar with a coffee filter or a piece of cloth secured with a rubber band.

Let the jar stand at warm room temperature, out of direct sunlight. You should start to see bubbles forming on the top within 1 to 5 days, depending on the temperature of your environment and the wild yeasts present.

Once the mixture is bubbly, stir it. Using a funnel, pour it into a bottle, leaving at least 1 inch (2.5 cm) of headspace. Cap the bottle and store it at room temperature for 1 to 5 days. When the soda is carbonated (see page 161), transfer the bottle to the refrigerator. Store in the refrigerator and drink within 2 weeks.

YIELD: 1/2 GALLON (2 L)

Sarsaparilla

SARSAPARILLA HAS LONG BEEN USED BY THE INDIGENOUS PEOPLES OF Central and South America and, like all root beers, it began its life as a health tonic. It's been used to support the urinary system and liver, to treat skin conditions and rheumatism, and as a remedy for syphilis. This recipe includes a little sassafras (*Sassafras albidum*) and wintergreen (*Gaultheria procumbens*) to round out the sarsaparilla (*Smilax ornata*) flavor without overpowering it.

SARSAPARILLA SODA BASE

6 tablespoons (¾ ounce, or 21 g) cut and sifted sarsaparilla root

1 tablespoon (¼ ounce, or 7 g) cut and sifted sassafras root bark

1 tablespoon (¼ ounce, or 7 g) cut and sifted wintergreen leaves

¼ cup (1½ ounces, or 42 g) raisins, coarsely chopped

3-inch (7.5 cm) piece vanilla bean, split lengthwise

1½ cups (355 ml) water

1 cup (225 g) packed brown sugar (such as jaggery or piloncillo)

Combine the sarsaparilla, sassafras, wintergreen, raisins, vanilla, and water in a saucepan. Cover and bring to a boil. Reduce the heat to low and simmer, covered, for 20 minutes. Strain the mixture through a fine-mesh strainer, pressing with the back of a spoon to extract all the liquid; discard the solids. Stir in the sugar. Let cool to room temperature. Follow the instructions below to make soda using either Champagne yeast or a ginger bug.

CHAMPAGNE YEAST FERMENTATION

THIS SODA MAKES A DELICIOUS FLOAT WHEN IT'S SERVED IN A TALL, frosty glass with a generous scoop of vanilla ice cream!

1 recipe Sarsaparilla Soda Base (above)

About 7 cups (1645 ml) lukewarm, unchlorinated water

⅛ teaspoon Champagne yeast

Using a funnel, pour the Sarsaparilla Soda Base into a bottle. Top off the bottle with the lukewarm water, leaving at least 1 inch (2.5 cm) of headspace. Add the yeast to the bottle.

Cap the bottle tightly and shake it well.

Store the bottle at room temperature, out of direct sunlight, for 1 to 3 days. When the soda is carbonated (see page 161), transfer the bottle to the refrigerator. Store in the refrigerator and drink within 2 weeks.

YIELD: ½ GALLON (2 L)

GINGER BUG FERMENTATION

I PREFER THE PURER FLAVOR OF THIS SODA WHEN IT'S MADE WITH Champagne yeast. But ginger can add warmth and spiciness, so try this soda in place of ginger ale in a rum-laden Dark and Stormy cocktail.

1 recipe Sarsaparilla Soda Base (page 168)
1 cup (235 ml) strained liquid from Ginger Bug Soda Starter (page 162)
About 6 cups (1410 ml) lukewarm, unchlorinated water

Combine the Sarsaparilla Soda Base and strained Ginger Bug Soda Starter in a wide-mouth, ½-gallon (2 L) jar. Top off the jar with the lukewarm water, leaving 1 inch (2.5 cm) of headspace. Give it a good stir. Cover the jar with a coffee filter or a piece of cloth secured with a rubber band.

Let the jar stand at warm room temperature, out of direct sunlight. You should start to see bubbles forming on the top within 1 to 5 days, depending on the temperature of your environment and the wild yeasts present.

Once the mixture is bubbly, stir it. Using a funnel, pour it into a bottle, leaving at least 1 inch (2.5 cm) of headspace. Cap the bottle and store it at room temperature for 1 to 5 days. When the soda is carbonated (see page 161), transfer the bottle to the refrigerator. Drink within 2 weeks.

YIELD: ½ GALLON (2 L)

Botanical Note: In 1960, the FDA banned the use of sassafras root bark in mass-produced food products, following a study in which lab rats developed cancer from being fed large doses of safrole, a constituent of sassafras oil. The amount of sassafras used in homemade soda is typically so small that you'd need to drink mass quantities of it in order to ingest the same level of safrole; however, if you're concerned, you can just omit the sassafras from this recipe and use more wintergreen instead.

Blueberry Soda

ANTIOXIDANT-RICH BLUEBERRIES TAKE CENTER STAGE HERE, WITH bright, tart lemon and aromatic cinnamon as supporting acts. (The cinnamon is optional, so if you're not a fan, feel free to skip it—but I think it really helps accentuate the blueberries' flavor.) Try making this refreshing soda with other berries, including blackberries, bilberries, huckleberries, and elderberries.

BLUEBERRY SODA BASE

1 quart (1 L) water

1 quart 1½ pounds, or 680 g) blueberries

1½ cups (300 g) sugar

Juice of 3 medium lemons (6 tablespoons, or 90 ml)

3-inch (7.5 cm) cinnamon stick (optional)

Bring the water to a boil in a large saucepan. Stir in the blueberries. Reduce the heat and simmer, uncovered, for 10 minutes. Remove from the heat and stir in the sugar, lemon juice, and cinnamon. Let cool to room temperature.

Strain the mixture through a fine-mesh strainer, gently pressing on the berries to extract the liquid, but without forcing the pulp through the strainer. Discard the solids, or save them for another use (topping yogurt, for instance). Follow the instructions below to make soda using either Champagne yeast or a ginger bug.

CHAMPAGNE YEAST FERMENTATION

SIP THIS SODA STRAIGHT UP IF YOU'RE IN THE MOOD FOR SOMETHING pure and fruity, or use it to add a unique flavor to cocktails like mojitos.

1 recipe Blueberry Soda Base (above)

About 4 cups (940 ml) lukewarm, unchlorinated water

⅛ teaspoon Champagne yeast

Using a funnel, pour the Blueberry Soda Base into a bottle. Top off the bottle with the lukewarm water, leaving at least 1 inch (2.5 cm) of headspace. Add the yeast to the bottle. Cap the bottle tightly and shake it well.

Store the bottle at room temperature, out of direct sunlight, for 1 to 3 days. When the soda is carbonated (see page 161), transfer the bottle to the refrigerator. Store in the refrigerator and drink within 2 weeks.

YIELD: ½ GALLON (2 L)

GINGER BUG FERMENTATION

BLUEBERRIES, GINGER, AND CINNAMON AREN'T JUST DELICIOUS; THEY also have anti-inflammatory properties. To make this soda even healthier, you could reduce the sugar in the Blueberry Soda Base recipe, and use an unrefined or less refined sugar in place of white sugar.

1 recipe Blueberry Soda Base (page 170)

1 cup (235 ml) strained liquid from Ginger Bug Soda Starter (page 162)

About 3 cups (705 ml) lukewarm, unchlorinated water

Combine the Blueberry Soda Base and strained Ginger Bug Soda Starter in a wide-mouth, ½-gallon (2 L) jar. Top off the jar with the lukewarm water, leaving 1 inch (2.5 cm) of headspace. Give it a good stir. Cover the jar with a coffee filter or a piece of cloth secured with a rubber band.

Let the jar stand at warm room temperature, out of direct sunlight. You should start to see bubbles forming on the top within 1 to 5 days, depending on the temperature of your environment and the wild yeasts present.

Once the mixture is bubbly, stir it. Using a funnel, pour it into a bottle, leaving at least 1 inch (2.5 cm) of headspace. Cap the bottle and store it at room temperature for 1 to 5 days. When the soda is carbonated (see page 161), transfer the bottle to the refrigerator. Store in the refrigerator and drink within 2 weeks.

Elderflower Fizz

IN ENGLAND, MOST PEOPLE USE THE NATURAL YEASTS PRESENT IN THE
air and on elderflower blossoms to make a delicately floral elderflower fizz or
"champagne." While this might sound ultra-romantic (at least to the fermentation
nerd!), I've found the wild yeast method to be hit or miss in terms of effectiveness
and ideal flavor. That's why I usually add a pinch of cultivated yeast to the mix at the
beginning, but I've included both options here in case you're in an adventurous
mood. Speaking of adventure, this is a notoriously explosive recipe—particularly
if your flowers are abundant in yeast—so be sure to use plastic bottles for this one.
Consider yourself forewarned.

3 to 6 elderflower heads, depending on size

Grated peel of 1 medium lemon (1 tablespoon, or 6 g)

Juice of 1 medium lemon (2 tablespoons, or 30 ml)

2½ teaspoons (23 ml) white wine vinegar

1¼ cups (250 g) sugar

½ gallon (2 L) water

⅓ teaspoon Champagne yeast (optional)

Gently shake the elderflower heads to remove any dirt or insects. Separate the flowers
from the stems, trying to remove as many of the stems as you can (a few are fine, but too
many can make you sick because they contain cyanide-inducing glycosides). Combine the
elderflowers, lemon peel, lemon juice, vinegar, sugar, and water in a large bowl or
fermenting crock. Stir well to dissolve the sugar.

If you want to kick-start the fermentation immediately, sprinkle the Champagne yeast
on top of the liquid. Otherwise, you can wait a couple of days to see whether it ferments
naturally. Cover the bowl with a clean kitchen towel and let stand at room temperature,
out of direct sunlight, for 2 days. If you didn't add yeast at the beginning, check for signs of
bubbles; if no bubbles are present, add the yeast at this time. Let stand for 2 more days.

Using a funnel lined with a flour sack towel, transfer the liquid into a bottle, leaving at
least 1 inch (2.5 cm) of headspace. Cap the bottle tightly. Discard the solids.

Store the bottle in a cool, dark place for 1 week, burping it daily. Transfer to the refrigerator and drink within 1 year.

YIELD: ¹/₂ **GALLON (2 L)**

Nettle Beer

NETTLE BEER HAS A TASTE REMINISCENT OF HARD CIDER WITH EARTHY,
slightly peppery notes. It's best made with fresh, young stinging nettle (*Urtica
dioica*) tops, clipped from the top few inches (5 to 7.5 cm) of the plant before it
goes to flower. I've also tried this with dried nettle and though dried nettle beer
isn't quite as good, it can provide the iron, calcium, and other minerals that nettle
is so prized for. Stinging nettle has also been used as a remedy for allergies and
hay fever.

8 ounces (227 g) fresh nettle tops or 4 ounces (112 g) dried
½ gallon (2 L) water
½ cup (96 g) turbinado or raw sugar
Juice of 1 lemon
¾ teaspoon ale yeast

Combine the nettles and water in a pot. Bring to a boil. Reduce the heat and simmer,
uncovered, for 15 minutes.

Place the sugar in a large bowl or fermenting crock. Line a fine-mesh strainer with flour
sack cloth and strain the nettle liquid into the bowl. When cool enough to handle, gather
the cloth around the nettles and squeeze to extract all the liquid. Stir to dissolve the sugar.
Let cool to room temperature. Stir in the lemon juice. Sprinkle the yeast on top of the liquid. Cover the bowl with a clean kitchen towel and let stand at room temperature, out of
direct sunlight, for 3 days.

Using a funnel with a fine-mesh sieve over it, transfer the liquid into a bottle, leaving at
least 1 inch (2.5 cm) of headspace. Cap the bottle tightly. Store it in a cool, dark place for 1
week, burping it daily. Transfer it to the refrigerator and drink within 1 year. When serving, pour carefully so that any sediment remains at the bottom of the bottle. Don't worry if
the beer is cloudy: it's simply a characteristic of home brews, and it's harmless.

YIELD: **¹/₂ GALLON (2 L)**

Basic Water Kefir

WATER KEFIR GRAINS NEED STEADY ATTENTION, BUT ONCE YOU GET THE hang of it, making water kefir can become an easy part of your regular routine. To flourish, the bacteria and yeast need unchlorinated, unfluoridated water and sugar. They also need minerals—and that means avoiding distilled water and, perhaps, giving them a little mineral supplementation. An unrefined sugar, a bit of molasses, or a little unsulfured dried fruit will give your water kefir grains the minerals they need. Don't use honey, coconut sugar, agave, or sugar substitutes, though. Honey has antimicrobial properties and coconut sugar is very rich, so they can weaken water kefir grains, while agave and sugar substitutes don't contain the nutrients that are necessary for the water kefir grains' survival. Keep in mind, too, that darker sugars will make a water kefir with a stronger flavor.

BASIC WATER KEFIR

1 quart (1 L) unchlorinated, unfluoridated water
¼ cup (50 g) cane sugar, such as white sugar, raw sugar, turbinado, or sucanat
2 tablespoons (20 g) water kefir grains
½ teaspoon blackstrap molasses, or 4 unsulfured raisins, or ½ unsulfured dried fig

Combine the water and sugar in a ½-gallon (2 L) jar. Cover the jar with a lid and shake it until the sugar dissolves. Remove the lid and add the water kefir grains to the jar. Add the molasses. Loosely cover the jar with a coffee filter, cloth, or hard lid.

Store the jar at warm room temperature, out of direct sunlight, and let it ferment for 48 hours. (If left longer than 48 hours, the grains may starve and disintegrate.) As it ferments, the water will turn cloudy and slightly bubbly, and it will start to taste less sweet than the original sugar water.

Prepare a new jar of sugar water, repeating the steps above. Strain the fermented water kefir through a fine-mesh strainer into a jar. Transfer the water kefir grains to the new jar of sugar water. The finished water kefir is now ready to be flavored and turned into soda.

YIELD: 1 QUART (1 L)

NOTE:
Water kefir grains can react with metals such as aluminum, so always use nonmetal or stainless steel strainers and other utensils.

WILD DRINKS AND COCKTAILS

Handling multiplying water kefir grains: After a few batches, water kefir grains will start to multiply. This can be exciting, but if they multiply quickly, it can be overwhelming. To keep the grains healthy, use no more than ¼ cup (40 g) of grains in 1 quart (1 L) of water. You can start a new jar of sugar water for the extra grains. Share them with friends, throw them into smoothies, or compost them.

Putting water kefir grains on hold: If you're going on vacation or want to take a break from making water kefir, you can put the grains to sleep. To store them for up to 1 month, place the grains in a new jar of sugar water, cover the jar with an airtight lid, and refrigerate. To store them for up to 6 months, rinse the grains in unchlorinated, unfluoridated water and lay them on a piece of parchment paper to dry for a few days. Transfer the dried grains to an airtight container and refrigerate. To reactivate the grains, transfer them to a new jar of sugar water and proceed as usual; it may take a few batches for them to wake up fully.

WATER KEFIR SODA

ALTHOUGH BASIC WATER KEFIR IS DRINKABLE, IT BECOMES MUCH MORE palatable when you turn it into a flavored soda. Enhance the kefir with tea, juice, syrup, or fruit; let the carbonation build for a day or three; and you have a refreshing and fizzy soda filled with healthful probiotics.

2½ cups (588 ml) finished Basic Water Kefir (page 174)
1½ cups (355 ml) flavored liquid (page 177)

Make sure any flavored liquid, such as an infusion, a decoction, or fruit juice, is completely cooled before using.

Using a funnel, pour the water kefir into a bottle. Fill the rest of the bottle with the flavored liquid, leaving at least 1 inch (2.5 cm) of headspace. Cap the bottle tightly and shake it well.

Store the bottle at room temperature, out of direct sunlight, for 12 to 72 hours. When the soda is carbonated (see page 161), transfer the bottle to the refrigerator. Store in the refrigerator and drink within 1 month.

YIELD: 1 QUART (1 L)

Use any of these flavored liquids in your water kefir sodas:

- **Strong herbal infusion** (see page 24) or decoction (see page 25): 1½ cups (355 ml) liquid sweetened with 2 to 3 tablespoons sugar (25 to 37.5 g) or honey (40 to 60 g).

- **Fruit juice** (to make fruit juice from scratch, see page 25): 1½ cups (355 ml) unsweetened juice

- **Syrup** (see examples in chapter 3): ¼ cup (60 ml) syrup combined with 1¼ cups (295 ml) water

- **Fruit-flavored water kefir:** ½ to 2 cups (75 to 300 g) chopped fruit per quart (1 L) water kefir

Grapefruit and Sage Water Kefir

MOST COMMERCIAL SODAS—AND EVEN HOMEMADE ONES—ARE TOO SWEET for me, so I'm a big fan of this Grapefruit and Sage Water Kefir. Its bittersweet taste is sophisticated and refreshing; plus, grapefruit is chock-full of vitamin C, while sage has been used in herbal medicine to support the liver, help digest fats, and sharpen the senses. Serve it straight up as a nonalcoholic aperitif before a meal or use it in pre-dinner cocktails, where it adds plenty of flavor and fizz without a hefty dose of sugar. Try it in a Paloma cocktail with tequila, or use it instead of wine in a spritz with a bitter liqueur like Calisaya or Campari.

Juice of 1 pink grapefruit (about ⅔ cup, or 160 ml)
Peel of 1 pink grapefruit, cut in wide strips
1 tablespoon (2.5 g) chopped fresh sage leaves
1 tablespoon (20 g) honey
3 to 3½ cups (705 to 825 ml) finished Basic Water Kefir (page 174)

Bring the grapefruit juice to a boil in a small saucepan. Remove from the heat and stir in the grapefruit peels, sage, and honey. Let stand for 1 hour. Strain the mixture through a fine-mesh strainer, pressing to extract all the liquid; discard the solids.

Using a funnel, pour the grapefruit mixture and Basic Water Kefir into a bottle, leaving at least 1 inch (2.5 cm) of headspace. Cap the bottle tightly and shake it well.

Store the bottle at room temperature, out of direct sunlight, for 12 to 72 hours. When the soda is carbonated (see page 161), transfer the bottle to the refrigerator. Store in the refrigerator and drink within 1 month.

YIELD: 1 QUART (1 L)

Variation: For a soda that's a bit more bitter, replace the sage with ¼ to ½ cup (2 to 4 g) dried hops flowers (*Humulus lupulus*).

Apple Cider Water Kefir

BOTH MY HUSBAND AND I LOVE SPARKLING HARD CIDER, BUT WE NEVER got into making homemade versions for a couple of reasons. First, true home-brewed cider, while delicious, can take many months to age, and we found that all the effort wasn't worth it, because we didn't have room to make and store more than a jug or two in our tiny apartment. We also tried making wild or "spontaneous" cider simply by leaving apple juice out to ferment (and there are folks who swear by this method). But this left us at the mercy of our wild yeasts, and, unfortunately, the results never tasted very good to us. Happily, this water kefir version of "hard cider" satisfies our palates and our desire for quicker, if not instant, gratification. It's lightly alcoholic—about 2 percent—pleasantly dry, and a snap to make.

4 cups (940 ml) apple cider or cloudy apple juice

2 tablespoons (20 g) water kefir grains

1 quart (1 L) unchlorinated, unfluoridated water

¼ cup (50 g) cane sugar, such as granulated sugar, raw sugar, turbinado, or sucanat

Combine the apple cider and water kefir grains in a ½-gallon (2 L) jar. Cover the jar with a coffee filter or a piece of cloth secured with a rubber band. Store the jar at warm room temperature, out of direct sunlight, and let it ferment for 24 to 48 hours. (Because of the high sugar content of the apple cider, the longer it ferments, the higher the alcohol content will be.)

Combine the water and sugar using the process on page 174. Strain the fermented apple cider through a fine-mesh strainer into a jar. Transfer the water kefir grains to the jar of sugar water. (To keep water kefir grains healthy, always give them a rest in plain sugar water after using them in a fruit juice fermentation.)

Using a funnel, pour the fermented apple cider into a bottle, leaving at least 1 inch (2.5 cm) headspace. Cap the bottle tightly. Store the bottle at room temperature, out of direct sunlight, for 12 to 48 hours. When the cider is carbonated (see page 161), transfer the bottle to the refrigerator. Store in the refrigerator and drink within 1 month.

YIELD: 1 QUART (1 L)

Variation: To make water kefir perry, simply replace the apple cider with unfiltered pear juice.

RESOURCES

Ingredients and Supplies

HERBS AND SPICES
Mountain Rose Herbs
www.mountainroseherbs.com

FRESH AND DRIED HERBS AND SEEDS
Pacific Botanicals
www.pacificbotanicals.com

SEEDS AND PLANTS
Horizon Herbs
www.horizonherbs.com

Crimson Sage Nursery
www.crimson-sage.com

HOME-BREWING SUPPLIES
Northern Brewer
www.northernbrewer.com

WATER KEFIR GRAINS
Kombucha Kamp
www.kombuchakamp.com

BOTTLES AND JARS
Specialty Bottle
www.specialtybottle.com

Books about Plants

Brill, "Wildman" Steve. *Identifying and Harvesting Edible and Medicinal Plants in Wild (and Not So Wild) Places* (William Morrow, 1994).

Elpel, Thomas J. *Botany in a Day: The Patterns Method of Plant Identification* (Hops Press, 2013).

Falconi, Dina. *Foraging and Feasting: A Field Guide and Wild Food Cookbook* (Botanical Arts Press, 2013).

Gladstar, Rosemary. *Rosemary Gladstar's Medicinal Herbs: A Beginner's Guide* (Storey Publishing, 2012).

Green, James. *The Herbal Medicine-Maker's Handbook: A Home Manual* (Crossing Press, 2000).

Petersen Field Guides, including *A Field Guide to Medicinal Plants and Herbs of Eastern and Central North America* by Steven Foster and James A. Duke (Houghton Mifflin Harcourt, 2014) and *A Field Guide to Western Medicinal Plants and Herbs* by Steven Foster and Christopher Hobbs (Houghton Mifflin Harcourt, 2002).

Sams, Tina. *Healing Herbs: A Beginner's Guide to Identifying, Foraging, and Using Medicinal Plants* (Fair Winds Press, 2015).

Thayer, Samuel. *Nature's Garden: A Guide to Identifying, Harvesting and Preparing Wild Edible Plants* (Forager's Harvest, 2010).

Tilford, Gregory L. *From Earth to Herbalist: An Earth-Conscious Guide to Medicinal Plants* (Mountain Press Publishing Company, 1998).

Timber Press's regional foraging books, including *California Foraging* by Judith Larner Lowry (2014); *Midwest Foraging* by Lisa M. Rose (2015); *Northeast Foraging* by Leda Meredith (2014); *Pacific Northwest Foraging* by Douglas Deur (2014); and *Southeast Foraging* by Chris Bennett.

Books about Drinks

Bobrow, Warren. *Apothecary Cocktails: Restorative Drinks from Yesterday and Today* (Fair Winds, 2013).

Christensen, Emma. *True Brews: How to Craft Fermented Cider, Beer, Wine, Sake, Soda, Mead, Kefir and Kombucha at Home* (Ten Speed Press, 2013).

Dietsch, Michael. *Shrubs: An Old-Fashioned Drink for Modern Times* (Countryman Press, 2014).

Katz, Sandor. *The Art of Fermentation*, 2003, and *Wild Fermentation*, 2012 (Chelsea Green Publishing).

Loeb, Katie M. *Shake, Stir, Pour: Fresh Homegrown Cocktails* (Quarry, 2012).

Parsons, Brad Thomas. *Bitters: A Spirited History of a Classic Cure-All* (Ten Speed Press, 2011).

Stewart, Amy. *The Drunken Botanist: The Plants That Create the World's Great Drinks* (Algonquin Books, 2013).

Educational Resources

American Herbalists Guild
www.americanherbalistsguild.com

LearningHerbs.com
learningherbs.com

National Center for Home
Food Preservation
nchfp.uga.edu

Plant Healer
planthealer.org

The Sustainable Herbs Project
www.numenfilm.com/blog/
sustainable-herbs

United Plant Savers
www.unitedplantsavers.org

USDA Cooperative Extension
System Offices
www.csrees.usda.gov/extension

USDA Plants Database
www.plants.usda.gov

ACKNOWLEDGMENTS

TO MY HUSBAND, GREGORY HAN: THANK YOU FOR BEING MY PARTNER IN exploring the natural world, and for your boundless patience, insight, and support as I filled our home with bottles and jars, made you taste all manner of concoctions at the oddest of hours, and asked you just "one more" question. I love you.

To my brother, Bruce Ho: I am enormously grateful for your expertise and steadfast support. To my parents, Mobi Warren, Hoang Ho, Philip Phillips, and Michelle Denyer: Thank you for teaching, encouraging, and inspiring me; you are the roots of my passion for cooking, nature, and healing. Thank you to Bruce Warren, Eleanor Han, James Phillips, and Lucas Denyer-Ho; I couldn't ask for a better family. I also want to acknowledge my beloved grandmothers, Vường Coi and Alma Jane Warren, whose spirits permeate my love for plants, animals, handiwork, and history.

Thank you to everyone at Quarto Publishing Group and Fair Winds Press, especially Jill Alexander, for envisioning and championing this book, and Winnie Prentiss, Heather Godin, Cara Connors, Alison Stone, Katie Fawkes, and Becky Gissel. And much appreciation to Amanda Richmond, Megan Buckley, and Karen Levy.

To Rebecca Altman: Thank you for your friendship and teaching, and for being the ying to my yang. To Kate Payne, Andrea Nguyen, Pamela Slim, and Rose Lawrence: I am so grateful for your encouragement and advice. To Grace Hsiu, Shane Redsar, Melanie McGraw, and Erin Cullerton, thank you for lending a hand!

To Matthew Biancaniello, Rosalee de la Forêt, and John Gallagher: Working with each one of you has taught and inspired me so much—thank you.

Deepest gratitude to my enthusiastic team of taste testers and recipe testers: Alex Chao, Andrea Lay, Angeline Woo, Anne Powell, Anouk Booneman, Anya Farquhar, Bethany Harris, Bill Garretson, Colleen O'Bryant, Dan Kitchens, Daniella de Vreeze, Ellen Demotses, Heather Hoffman, Jayme Henderson, Jenny Suh, Jess Collins, Julie James, Karen Hobert, Kassia Shaw, Katie Bergin, Kozy Kitchens, Kristen Schaffenberger Davis, Krystal Chang, Lania Cortez, Laura Fletcher, Laura Loewen, Leah Vautrot, Louis Changchien, Mandy Gough, Marissa Harrington, Martin Cendreda, Michele Graham, Nick Kimpton, Raylene McCalman, Roshni Kavate, Sascha Bos, Susan Lutz, Tabby Nanyonga, Tanya Thampi Sen, and Vicki Karlan. And thank you to Mike Hawthorn, Sharin Cooper, and Kathleen Sanchez for your generosity as wildcrafters.

Finally, thank you to all of my teachers, students, editors, and readers over the years. I would not be here without you.

ABOUT THE AUTHOR

EMILY HAN EMPOWERS PEOPLE TO CULTIVATE a mindful relationship with nature and nourishment. As a writer, recipe developer, and educator, she focuses on topics such as handmade food and drinks, foraging and wildcrafting, and herbs and spices. She is the founder of L.A. Food Swap and cofounder of the International Food Swap Network. In addition to apprenticeships in herbalism and cocktail crafting, she studied art history at Hampshire College, library science at San José State University, and food preservation at University of California Cooperative Extension. Emily lives in Los Angeles with her two cats and her husband Gregory, with whom she spends every opportunity exploring the mountains, deserts, and beaches of Southern California.

To learn more, visit http://emilyhan.com.

INDEX

WILD DRINKS AND COCKTAILS